Save for Fireflies

Home on the Roads across America

A Travel Memoir

NATHANIEL MISSILDINE

Save for Fireflies: Home on the Roads Across America

Copyright © Nathaniel Missildine, 2012
All rights reserved

No part of this book may be reproduced, copied or used in any form, electronic or otherwise, without the prior written consent of the copyright owner, excepting quotations for review or other critical articles.

Portions of this book originally appeared online at
www.thenervousbreakdown.com

ISBN 978-1-4709-2914-5

to Julie and Louise

FIDGETING - - -

This was how it actually happened. I fell for a girl who wasn't from around here. She had bluish-gray eyes that changed depending on the light, a knack for making strangers feel like long-lost friends and a habit of insisting that all the hangers in a closet face the same way. She viewed the world positively and forgave quickly. She spoke English with mistakes that I never wanted to correct such as assigning gender pronouns to inanimate objects or pronouncing the word "puddle" with a long "u" sound, so that after a rainstorm, we were constantly stepping around "poodles."

I realized the rest of my life had started one night after I dropped her off. I drove back alone on a westbound street in San Francisco. A fog had lifted. "This," I said aloud, "you should keep."

As we settled into a life together, Cecile came to me with news that would spin us into another orbit. Immigration services had tightened visa policies, as part of a host of restrictions being put in place at the tail-end of 2001. Her work visa would soon expire and, despite her company formally stating her as invaluable, she was refused any chance of renewal. She was forced to leave the United States. Our timing with the rest of the world was, not for the last time, off.

SAVE FOR FIREFLIES

She returned to her native France by the end of the year. It didn't take me long to come around to the decision to follow her. We moved to Paris and, shortly after, settled down in the city of Dijon, France, her hometown. We married and started a family, ushering into the world two dynamo-powered French-American girls. Four years passed in a kind of antique carousel whirl of pink booties and pureéd carrots set to the sounds of a foreign language I was gradually embracing. I came to feel comfortable in a country I'd always viewed as a panoramic postcard. I went to sleep at night wondering how I'd ended up *ici*, of all places.

I knew I couldn't have imagined a better turn of events if I'd sat down to drunkenly, wildly daydream toward the clouds. I was happy.

Still, after all this high adventure, I wasn't yet ready for total stasis. Having reached the end of our beginning, I found myself struck with the nagging impulse to look back.

Nostalgia, by now, should have become irrelevant. But I couldn't tear myself away. I turned my gaze to what I'd left. I made a list from our sunny apartment in Dijon.

What I Then Missed
* free refills
* loudmouths
* humor as an extension of sincerity and trust
* hysterics
* renewal rising from calamity and chaos
* roomy interiors
* Fritos
* fireflies

The ex-patriot experience is well documented. France, for one, has been puzzled over by Anglos for centuries now. Countless writers have tried to make sense of this hexagonal nation in particular. But, I wasn't interested in adapting to the culture by chronicling my impressions of its quirks and eccentricities. Instead, my curiosity drifted back.

I suffered flutters of homesickness inside tight interiors. I had nothing resembling a Frito available to me, nor available loud or hysterical persons to use as a sounding board for my own oddness. I longed for the drama of my fellow citizens. I yearned for people who recognized jokes as a gesture of kindness. My thirst was never quenched without free refills. Still, I could make do on most of these accounts.

But it was the fireflies I couldn't get over. Reportedly, the firefly exists in France, though I've never seen one. I've often found myself staring out of our third story window at sunset, double checking for the bugs of my summers past. One night, I caught instead a distant whiff of a late August mid-Atlantic evening when the humidity of the day cooled into a twilight breeze that blew across the lawn my father had just mowed and into our screened-in porch. I wanted to stand on a lawn just like it while fireflies winked over the trimmed and freshly lighter green grass. I wanted to be able to catch one in my hand.

I needed to be reminded that the modest places where fireflies appeared at dusk were still there, that I could, whenever I may so please, take my daughters to them. I needed to know that this and a hundred other little splendors I'd fixed in my mind as specific to my native country hadn't disappeared, that the cogs of the communities of my upbringing still turned, and that someone, somewhere among them had saved me a spot.

Before I was able to acknowledge it, I was, as the French say, *pas dans mon assiette*. Not in my own plate. My learning of the language plateaued and my desire to seamlessly fit into a European way of life waned. I began fidgeting like one of my daughters strapped too long into a car seat.

Full-blown identity crises were part of the living overseas package. Being abroad meant trying to dismiss a low-level ache of loneliness and acceptance of never casually belonging. As my girls grew, picking up not just the French language, but its customs and cultural nuances with much more ease than I ever did, the ache spread. I explained what was missing to my folks back home one afternoon, early morning their time. It was then I heard myself say the following "The U.S. fascinates me from over here. It's really *terrible*."

Confused silence met me on the other end. I had done two alarming things. First, I'd pronounced the word "terrible" the French way: "terREEbluh." Second, I'd used the word the French way, where "terrible" can, depending on the context, be positive.

This wasn't the first time I'd let French spill into English. But where before it may have been funny or sophisticated (I'd once called a suitcase a *valise* to an unamused Philadelphia airport worker), this time was different. During this conversation, at this bend in the arc of my life in France, the *terrible* mistake rattled me to the core. I wanted off this continent. I had the overwhelming urge to hop on the next train to the airport for a one-way ticket back across the ocean. After my five-year effort of adapting to a foreign land, what place did I have in the one I'd grown up in? Would my U.S. passport be revoked now that I was saying things like *terreebluh*? How would my little girls ever master any language when their father didn't appear to have a full grasp on one? Had either of them ever even seen a firefly? Would they recognize one as real if it lit up before their eyes?

I'd reached a four-lane crossroads, growing comfortable in fatherhood while hearing a train whistle the final departure of youth. At that same time, I also suffered from an acute bout of expatriate unease while witnessing my own metastasizing Euro-ness. And all of it was converging amidst a steady rise in public chatter that America was in decline. The possibility had arisen that it might not always be there to retreat back to.

Drastic measures were required. I purchased a guidebook to my own native country. I'd start with the wilderness. We'd need a year to plan the kind of trip I had in mind.

But by then, the journey that would take Cecile, our two small daughters and me in a camper van on a full circle around the highways and byways of the contiguous United States had already begun.

SAVE FOR FIREFLIES

REVENIR - - -

I unfolded a poster-size U.S. map over our kitchen table in Dijon one morning. Cecile and I stared down at the tangled network of red and black lines criss-crossing the pink landmass.
"What about White Sands, New Mexico? That's a place I'd like to visit." I pointed to the southwest corner of the map.
"Yeah. Okay. Why not?" she responded, noncommittal.
"As far as the route we'll take, I was thinking we'd start in Boston, head south and then west toward the desert and…"
"Wait. What are you doing?"
"I'm trying to work out the itinerary for the trip. So we can start planning."
"Yes, but that's not important right now."
"What d'you mean? We've got to work out a schedule. I wanted to go ahead and mark a date for each city we wanted to stop in."
"Marking dates?"
"Then we could estimate how many days we'd stay in each place."
"I don't want a schedule. We can figure things out as we go." She got up for another cup of coffee. This indicated she was done with the conversation.

"Right, but with the girls we need certain things planned out."

"No, no. No certain places, no certain times."

"I was going to make up a spreadsheet."

"Let me say my idea about this."

"Yes, please."

She folded up the map and handed it to me. "I want to eat asphalt."

"You want to eat it?"

"I want to conquer the road. I want to move."

"We're not running a race," I paused. "Are we?"

"I want the trip to be about seeing everything."

"When you say everything..."

"I'm planning on getting a new trip hat." Her mind was wandering.

"A hat?"

We had Cecile to thank for this time-off. She'd earned a three-month sabbatical, a much needed break from the pressure-cooker world of business public relations that she'd immersed herself in each weekday for the past twelve years. For me, the writer and the stay-at-home Dad, and for our girls, then ages two and four and a half, the days had their own separate kind of pressure. Still, at home, I didn't need to accrue vacation days.

Cecile was also hard-wired for epic voyages. Beginning around the time she was four, her family crossed the Sahara desert, hiked through the jungles of Southeast Asia, and once spent an entire year exploring and living in South America. They'd traveled to Turkey, China, all corners of Europe and most of Africa. They even braved the wilds of the United States of America. In fact, not only has Cecile visited far more countries of the world than I, but she has set foot in more U.S. states than I have. Taken together, all this continent-traversing has made Cecile resourceful, good with languages, uncomfortable with conformity and deathly allergic to standing still. On this trip, Cecile looked forward most to leaving the days open, while my idea was to organize the extended vacation making reservations and arrangements along our plotted course.

Though I wasn't quite ready to admit she was right, I realized I'd missed a larger purpose. The gut-level thrill of taking a trip like this one was the near total removal of constraints- of time, of place, of daily routine. For the first summer since we were kids, we wouldn't have to check a calendar or clock. The thrust of the trip then had little to do with the country I was currently in. I'd already caught myself entertaining visions of taking an off-ramp somewhere to an exit marked "Scenic Road Next 20 Miles." This was not something I should be assigning a pre-arranged date and time to.

This is the case with most any vacation. Being unbound is why we leave. Any housewife knows the grind that needs to be escaped. Househusbands know it perhaps more painfully. For this reason, many Dads at home also resort to writing about it.

At home, the days are regimented into unbending blocks of time. The monotony is your corrupt, megalomaniacal CEO. You stand in front of your kitchen cupboards wondering what in God's name you're going to make for dinner. Something quick and healthy and easy to clean up that the kids will love. You have to haul out the same pots and pans again that you just washed from lunch. Then, your task is to get the food into the kids' mouths involving sometimes intense negotiations, then to bed after a book and a song and a drink of water requested fifteen minutes after you turned off the light, then up in the morning and out the door in time for school because you've got a day of folding the same little socks into neat piles ahead of you (again) and now it looks like mildew is growing in the shower which you'll need to be on your knees scrubbing before it's time to get the little one, who has developed a cough in the two hours since you last saw her that you should probably make a doctor's appointment for just to be on the safe side, but before then it's lunchtime where you'll be back to the cupboards for more staring and pondering the exact same question you didn't have a good answer to yesterday.

  The kids are wonderful; mine teem with a particular magic that astonishes me more at each growth spurt. But the everydayness involved in doing all these necessary things for the angels that have chosen to take up residence in my house can be crushing. There is also the cruel mix of tedium and stress that is the hallmark of office jobs, which I've also spent time sampling. However, something about housework has a twisted endlessness that requires a patience and inner fortitude like no other job in the world.

  This line of work had occupied the past four years of my life and in a country where the product for scrubbing off that shower mildew was called, not Mr. Clean, but Monsieur

Propre (the same bald man on the label though). It meant my cabin fever had gotten just as fierce as my homesickness.

So when Cecile said "eating the asphalt," even if it was an idiom of her own invention, I understood. We would just go. Still I had questions for her before we concluded our trip-planning discussion.

"So we'll go beserk and just wing the whole trip?"

"How about this, you plan the places, the itinerary - whatever that means - and the dates and all this. Do a spreadsheet if you wish. But I want to know nothing."

"You want to show up to a campsite and be surprised to find our name on the reservation list?"

"Yes! I would love this."

Sea to shining sea it would be then. We would cover the ground, hoping to marry spontaneity with preparation, like a star-crossed couple still obviously destined for one another. We would go. Eating as much asphalt as we could sink our teeth into.

- - -

My own country existed now as a blank slate. I could roam anywhere within a long lost home of mine, without a fixed address around which to orient myself or offer reminders that the problems and marvels of America were concrete and lived daily. My parents' new home came close to a kind of launching pad, and theirs was the address I'd provided to border control at the airport when asked where I'd be staying. But no part of America was mine anymore. I had been afforded the chance to be a tourist in my own backyard, a curious guest in my own home.

We would be renting an RV that would serve as our roving house for the summer. We required something that could sleep the four of us with a minimum of comfort. We needed a place for two car seats and we probably couldn't do without a toilet, sink, fridge and stove. Additionally, we also wanted a motorhome on the smaller side that could fit into an average parking space without the use of semaphore signalers for the driver and didn't measure its gas consumption as gallons per mile.

Amenities and options have never been hard to come by in the American auto world. But as in a number of categories, we have size issues. A space-saving and scaled-down RV capable of sleeping four is a rarity. The well-known chains in the RV rental business tend toward motorhomes that ranged in sizes from shuttle bus to ocean liner and included billboard-sized advertisements for their rental companies emblazoned across the units. These are the 30+ foot long machines that come with an option of two gas tanks. On the inside, they sport full baths with showers and bathtubs, a living room and rec room with La-Z-Boy style armchairs, queen-sized beds and multiple television sets powered by droning generators. These RVs feature more square footage than most apartments I'd lived in and encourage their occupants not to exit the vehicle after having steamrolled into nature. We wanted to avoid these road dinosaurs if only to make venturing into nature our priority. We could handle minor inconveniences.

After consulting various agencies and dealers, we learned that the ideal model would be a Class B motorhome, often referred to as a camper van. It wasn't much more cumbersome than a typical family minivan. More importantly, these units sometimes averaged around 18 miles to a gallon, an anomaly among most RVs that offer less than half that. Since we weren't earnest enough to seek out one of a new breed of green RVs that ran on vegetable oil, nor would we be purchasing one of the many compact campers popular in Europe and having it shipped across just for the trip, we decided on the Class B. In the Northeast, the only location I found that rented a Class B motorhome suited for four was in the town of Peekskill, New York, an hour north of Manhattan.

I had a chance to visit during a hurried holiday trip home prior to our grand voyage. I'd selected our camper in Peekskill. Despite the disorganization of the agency and the vaguely distracted air of its owner and primary contact, Ernst, it didn't take long for me to shelve doubts. I took the details and photos of the camper back to Cecile and immediately signed and faxed the initial deposit for a ten-week long summer rental.

I tend to underestimate my ability to ignore sneaking suspicions. The visit to the rental agency didn't actually reassure me. Instead, it simply confirmed that I'd made the decision beforehand. As long as I was able to verify that the vehicle existed and looked like it did in the photo, it would probably have been a go. Any risks weren't worth taking the time to sift through. I'm not certain if it took an open-mouthed stupidity or a broader wisdom to assume early on that everything about living out of this moving house would go exactly as we planned and so fervently hoped.

- - -

The RV community calls it "hitch itch." One of a host of new terms I came to learn and understand first-hand as I researched mobile home life, hitch itch describes the feeling that your bricks-and-mortar life has become hopelessly bland, as you find yourself conjuring images of an open highway. Sitting still has become difficult and you look out the window of your kitchen wondering why the view hasn't changed. The road, four wheels and an elevated driver's seat are now whispering to you.

The narrator of Melville's Moby Dick, after insisting that we call him Ishmael, describes the moment he loses patience with his familiar surroundings "…whenever it requires a strong moral principle to prevent me from deliberately stepping into the street and methodically knocking people's hats off – then I account it high time to get to the sea as soon as I can."

Whether it was hitch-itch or a possible hell-bent chase for an existential sea creature, I accounted it high time myself to get out there as soon as I could.

Plus, summer turned up again. The kickoff to this celebrated season usually reminds me of all the summers that have come before it. It's always something of shocker to realize you can walk outside without a coat, and in short-sleeves, mind you. A day in April arrives where the weather decides to give up its harassment. The warm air settles in and a schools-out feeling begins to seep into the afternoons.

Around late April of that year, I opened the windows of our apartment in Dijon and the smell of summer poured into the room. Some small part of it must have sailed over to me from an open prairie or a rocky mountain or a mowed suburban lawn. *J'arrive,* I answered back.

We had two weeks until our trip. Time was slowing down as we approached the departure date. The gears of our clocks ticked as though they'd been filled with molasses. The wait was painful.

I primed our daughters. Our older daughter, Julie, then age four and a half, had always enjoyed car rides and plane trips and spoke of her upcoming travels like an old world explorer. "Do you know where I am soon going?" she would ask her friends, "America," she almost whispered. Her friends' eyes went wide. She might as well have said off to Neverland to fight Captain Hook and live with the Lost Boys.

Our younger daughter, Louise, having just attained age two, had no idea what lay in store. But she could sense the anticipatory hubbub. I didn't know whether to feel excited for her or deeply concerned.

One thing in our favor was that they both had always enjoyed riding in a car. Though not without moments of whining, long drives had a calming effect on Julie and Louise. To ensure they didn't lose this affinity for car travel, we drove frequently around the countryside on days off leading up to the trip.

I also wanted to instill in them a minimum hardiness for the outdoors. They both loved animals and had an unprodded interest in nature, but they weren't exactly rough-and-tumble. Skinned knees were still cause for great wails to the heavens and daylong fussing over the "boo-boo."

That spring, Louise sat at the top of the slide in the park, staring blankly down the metallic chute. She liked climbing the ladder and she enjoyed the view from the perch at the top, but sliding by herself remained something she was just not prepared to do. I would egg her on and then nudge her downward, but this only caused her to balk more. A line of other kids always formed behind her. I would take her by both hands, providing the security she craved, and she'd make the plunge with me. As for Julie, she loved movement, but still got fatigued easily on long strolls through town, often asking to be carried while dangling her limp arms toward the ground, like she'd just been forced to run a marathon. "You're getting too old for this," I'd say during my own moments of flagging patience. They needed a unique jumpstart.

Meanwhile, I'd hauled out the suitcase well in advance. Cecile, who typically asks herself at midnight what she'll bring for a plane trip the next day, slapped her hand on her forehead when she heard the sound coming from the bedroom of the unclasping baggage locks more than a week before our departure date.

I also delved into packing lists.

Essential Travel Items
* swimsuits
* clothes and shoes for all seasons, emphasis on extra socks and long sleeve T-shirts
* linens
* Ziploc bags
* mix tapes (kids and adult songs for our camper which had no CD player)
* first-aid kit
* hand sanitizer
* two "*doudous*", the French word for a child's favorite cuddle toy
* picture books, puzzles and coloring books
* Cecile's laptop
* two cell phones with international service
* a Swiss-army knife
* four pocket flashlights
* two car seats
* two hand-made nametags that read, "My name is Julie/Louise. If lost please contact this number…" written in both French and English
* six passports (a French and American one apiece for each of the girls)
* sugarless lollipops

Other lists that followed:

Things To Do Before Leaving France
* print out boarding passes
* turn off fridge

* do all procrastinated loads of laundry
* store away valuables
* drop keys off with in-laws
* arrange for mail pickup and plant watering
* drink wine and eat fresh soft cheese for cheap
* enjoy fully reimbursed doctor's visits and prescriptions
* savor fresh boulangerie bread
* send emails to notify friends just what the hell we were doing

Reasons I Wouldn't be Live-Blogging The Trip Despite Numerous Inquiries from Others
* needed a vacation from my computer
* needed to have an experience without first pondering how I'd be describing it
* didn't want to approach new people and places as only an observer
* sneaking suspicion there wouldn't be all that much down time
* wanted a record of the trip that took the completed, long view rather than the day-by-day
* because the glow of a campfire and the glow of a laptop screen should never be made to compete
* because a notebook and a campfire instead have an almost symbiotic relationship
* because routinely reporting how the trip's going allows less opportunity for it to change the traveler
* or for the experience to take shape as its own story

Reserved Campsites Cecile Was Willfully Uninformed Of
* Big Meadows campground, Shenandoah National Park, VA
* City of Rocks State Park campground, near Deming, NM
* Fernow Cabin, Coconino National Forest near Flagstaff, AZ
* Lodgepole campground, Sequoia National Park, CA
* Moraine campground, Rocky Mountain National Park, CO

Quotations To Heed
* "I discovered that I did not know my own country." - John Steinbeck, Travels with Charley
* "The worst thing about a trip like yours is having the kids with you at all times. The best thing about a trip like yours is having the kids with you at all times." - my father-in-law
* "Optimism is necessary in this country for social peace and economic prosperity." – Simone de Beauvoir, L'Amerique au jour de jour (America Day by Day)
* "A child of five could understand this. Send someone to fetch me a child of five." – Groucho Marx

SAVE FOR FIREFLIES

IGNITION - - -

Louise, didn't run, she galloped. That June she'd been walking for a mere six months, something of a late bloomer in this case which worried everyone except her parents. Her walking clicked one day and, in those months, she'd made up for the lost time. She'd learned how to keep up with her older, faster sister, though not by flat-out running, but rather in this patented gallop.

Louise kept her left leg in front, as the guide and the balance, while the back leg pushed her forward and up. She employed the arms too, raising them on each trot, not unlike Monty Python's King Arthur with hands out in front holding the reins of a horse that wasn't actually there. It also was obvious to anyone watching that she wasn't only using this gallop as a means of moving quickly; she simply enjoyed the stride itself. With each gallop, Louise would add a short squeal before landing both feet on the ground again.

Louise galloped on the late morning in June down the wide, polished concourse of Charles de Gaulle airport ahead of her sister and parents. Her curly head, bobbed with the motion, leading the way. She had a checkered pink backpack strapped over her shoulders. The weight of the Playmobil figures and select board books inside didn't stop her from keeping pace with the stampede of clomping shoes and wheeled Samsonite suitcases, big enough to house her entire body without bending her knees.

Louise only knew that she was going somewhere and was so thrilled to be going there with us and all these fine people with their impressive luggage. I had the sense then that it wouldn't be the last time on the trip that I'd draw my own courage from my children's optimism in what lay around the corner and their unconditional trust in my ability to get them to it.

So she galloped straight to the large windows and she and Julie both stopped to press their faces to the glass. We'd managed to get all our things into two large suitcases and a couple carry-ons, which we squeezed into the overhead bins upon boarding the plane. We were at last about to part ways with a fixed life.

We settled into our seats in the cabin, taking full advantage of the people-traveling-with-small-children-board-first rule. Once we were all situated in our row, with Cecile and I in the aisle seats and the girls together in the middle, an announcement from the flight crew informed us of a delay. They'd gotten word from the tower that all flights were momentarily grounded. It would be approximately a half-hour wait until a flight path could be cleared. The captain saved the cause of delay until the end. As our flight to the U.S. was about to disembark, George W. Bush and Air Force One were in the process of landing. This blocked all flights coming or going until they'd landed safely. The collective sigh from the cabin had more than the ordinary snark to it.

Here was a *bonjour* from my President. I couldn't help think how thoughtful it was of him. It seemed fitting that the man who'd made it that much harder to be an American abroad these past five years would make himself an inconvenience at the moment I attempted my return.

What was he doing in France? Soon to be unemployed, maybe he was on a three-month road trip through the French countryside. Or maybe he'd just been exiled, in time for us to breathe easy as we navigated our way through the lower forty-eight without his presence there. I was feeling hopeful.

- - -

Jamaica Plain, New York is somehow not one of the country's top tourist destinations. But the night before jumping into road travel at a hotel near Kennedy airport, the surroundings were dazzling enough. Likewise, the otherwise bland experience of eating burgers and chicken fingers (and free refills with ice cubes that needn't be requested) at the hotel restaurant, called The Great American Grill, was an exotic and lovely mini-odyssey. The refills and the pellet-sized ice cubes came in plastic red Coke glasses with bendy straws for everyone, even the two adults. The Great American Grill staff, entirely Pakistani, were welcoming and helpful.

I'd forgotten the convivial atmosphere of the country. I'd also forgotten how in public places Americans love to set the air conditioning to arctic frost. It felt like we were eating inside a refrigerator. The girls needed to put on sweaters. I stepped outside just to get a breath of warm air.

At the hotel entrance, hulking four-wheel-drive trucks and SUVs pulled under the hotel's entryway and guests emerged dressed in mismatched outfits, like a baseball cap with a suit jacket or an attractive, polished woman with expensive jewelry wearing sweatpants and white sneakers. In the lobby, a theater-size plasma screen broadcast a news channel crowded with on-screen graphics and two running tickers at the bottom before an empty faux living-room arrangement. The woman at the front desk greeted people with a smile, like they were friends, but also a generous helping of suspicion, like they could just as easily be arsonists there to burn the building down. Perhaps, she, like me, had seen too many movies.

In her book, America Day by Day (*L'Amérique au jour le jour*), Simone de Beauvoir describes her first night in New York City before an adventurous cross-country trip she took in 1947. She visits someone in a Manhattan apartment building and finds little details surreal, like the sound and shape of the doorbell, and it reminds of her of what she'd seen in films. "What disconcerts me is that those movie sets that I'd never really believed in are suddenly real," she observes. I now had more in common with her experience than any of the people unloading baggage from their colossal, shining cars. The content of my dear memories was suddenly just as cinematic and at the same time, for five hours already, just as real.

We were all unhinged and delirious from the flight, from our internal clocks telling us it was 1 a.m. and from free-floating, collective giddiness. Julie and I managed a quick visit to the pool, where her smile never faded. We returned to the room afterward, to find both Cecile and Louise in the same bed, fast asleep, with the table lamps still on. We washed and dried up and Julie immediately joined them.

I, however, returned to the hotel lobby. I took a seat in the armchair before that impressive plasma screen, now airing the NBA basketball playoffs and showcasing an old, bi-coastal rivalry between the Boston Celtics and L.A. Lakers. The players from here looked monstrous, the crowd smart and spring-loaded and the whole spectacle as majestic as anything I'd laid eyes on in recent memory. I was starting to lose certain key cognitive functions, but I wouldn't be able to sleep for at least another hour.

The next day, Ernst welcomed us to Peekskill and his humble rental lot. As the guy responsible for all that transpired at the RV rental agency, he was yet more distracted than he was during my last visit with him when I'd inspected the camper. He greeted us with the information that the vehicle we'd reserved was no longer available due to an engine problem. Instead they had another of the same motorhome with more miles on it and no shower. We were encouraged to make ourselves comfortable inside this switched vehicle in the meantime because Ernst still needed to straighten some things out.

I threw up my hands. Ernst apologized for the inconvenience. Since it was lunchtime by this point, we bought sandwiches at a nearby deli. With no park or nearby tables to sit down to, we took Ernst's suggestion to eat inside the camper. He popped his head in as we unwrapped our sandwiches over the back table.

"Very good, just stay where you are. The mechanics will be changing the tires now. Enjoy!" he said in his German accent.

So we ate our first meal inside the camper van while it was suspended on a hydraulic lift. The view out of the window was onto utility shelves of Valvoline bottles and grease-spotted walls of the agency's repair shop. Julie stood up on the back bench and peered out with her hands pressed to the glass.

"We're high up, Daddy."

"Yes."

"Why is that man taking pieces of our camping car?"

"We get new tires. While we have lunch. How about that?"

"That's nice of him."

Cecile meanwhile was opening and shutting cabinets around the sink area.

I turned to her. "I'm going to tell this guy to forget it. There's another rental agency I had as a back up in New Jersey. It would only postpone our plans for a day or two."

Cecile wasn't listening to me, or had tuned me out. She inspected the bucket seats and the kitchen area. "Oh this will be perfect."

"What?"

"We can store the food up here and the utensils on the bottom...and look, a magazine rack!"

Louise began testing the light switch buttons she could reach. Julie found, and promptly christened, the in-house potty. Everyone had already moved in.

Our house had four bucket seats, two in the front cabin and two in the rear beside large tinted windows ideal for scenic viewing that could hold car seats. Behind the driver's side seats was the closet with the small port-a-potty, smelling of only chemicals. On the passenger side was the two-burner gas stove, the refrigerator and a sink, along with various overhead compartments, all mini-versions of what comes in a typical home. The back area had the table with two benches on either side that converted into a double bed. There was also a temperature climate control panel, function labels in German. The bed for the girls was located in the cabover area, above the heads of the driver and front passenger. It was a crawlspace just their size. I surveyed the whole thing, testing the *auf* and *ab* switches. I realized that, despite things not going precisely as promised or planned, I should come around as well.

A 2002 Dodge Van Cruiser Royale would be our ride and our residence. The camper touched back down to the pavement. I asked Ernst why all this was just being done now. He had no real answer but offered to waive return fees. I asked if there were any other problems I should know about. "Nope, everything's fine now," he grinned, handing me the keys. Again, a suspicion shivered through me and, as before, I dismissed it, though not without more psychological effort.

"Remember don't go to Death Valley. Or the Yukon Territory. It's in the contract." Ernst was right; there was an arbitrary stipulation that Death Valley, California and areas in the Yukon Territory were strictly forbidden to enter with these rental units.

"Oh I'm sure we have plenty else to worry about."

On this trip, we really had no concrete destination. The endpoint would be the completion of an unimaginable loop that would bring us back to this very spot with the vehicle, and its passengers, still intact.

So we rolled onto the highway with the new tires, a full tank of the most expensive gasoline I'd ever purchased on U.S. soil and the soundtrack from Cinderella playing the song "A Dream is A Wish Your Heart Makes" getting the girls more revved up than anyone would have ever imagined. I, meanwhile, thought I heard a rumbling noise coming from under the hood and a squeaking sound from a loose part somewhere in the back. The steering wheel also felt strange and the gas pedal not as responsive. I had no idea if any of it was normal. In a few hours, I'd discover that the left headlight was out. But it was a little late to bother with any of it now.

I was getting into the music.

- - -

Connecticut was the first new state we entered, no more than five miles out of Peekskill. My mother, who'd attended school at UConn, heard this would be our first stretch of road said, "I'm so sorry. Just try to get through it as quickly as possible."

The Nutmeg State may represent the worst of the crowded and overpriced Northeast to some, but we sailed up I-84 through miles of blooming greenery. We zipped through the town of Waterbury and then slowed into rush hour traffic around Hartford, both times looking down onto the cities from the elevated highway overpasses, at the same height as the tops of the downtown buildings. Julie looked up at the gold dome of the Hartford state capitol and said, "Hey, look a castle!" It's one of the many hazards of growing up in Europe: you see castles in everything.

Before we took to nature, we had people to catch up with. Cecile's longtime friends from her college days, Yann and Sophie had lived in the U.S. for almost fifteen years and had two girls of their own, close in age to ours, with a third on the way. They had done the reverse of my experience, as French citizens in this part of the world. They'd both gotten jobs; she in marketing and he in finance. They'd made the adjustment to a new country without the support I had, with no native spouse to run interference and no in-laws or extended family nearby to lend help.

They lived in the wooded suburban community of Reading, north of Boston. We pulled into their driveway, parking beside their Dodge Durango and stepped into their colonial-style house with its large fenced-in yard where Yann was cooking marinated chicken on the grill. Their girls emerged bedecked in Dora the Explorer clothes and Sophie followed, more slowly as she was then six months pregnant. It was a very pleasant and very conventional American family scene. In fact, it all appeared to me more characteristically American than most households of

American friends I knew. It came as a surprise, then, when I heard *"Bonjour, comment ça va?"* and received a French bisous on both of my cheeks. *"Viens, Julie, on va jouer la bas,"* their eldest daughter chirped and all the girls skipped off to the toys.

"So Nat, how do you like living with the French?" Yann asked me, scowling on the word French.

"That depends. How are you dealing with all these ridiculous Americans?" I replied. This kicked off a brief litany of potshots at our own nations; I talked about the shallowness of America and he about the whiny French.

We generalized for the sake of argument and it was half out of politeness that we didn't lash into the other's culture, because there is no escaping the pride in your own heritage, no matter how many flaws you may see in it and, chiefly, because they may also be our own. Our wives were more willing to see the positive from both sides.

We touted life in France for these two who never lived as adults in their native country. We recounted details of the health care system like the fully reimbursed doctor housecalls in the dead of night and ubiquitous, knowledgably staffed and federally funded French pharmacies. We reminded them of well-maintained highways and the convenient and reliable nationwide train system. We told tales of cheap city-subsidized daycare and public schools flush with money that provided classes starting at age three. We mentioned the single commercial break during an hour-long t.v. program and the term I never fail to find miraculous: government subsidized arthouse movie theaters.

So what were the advantages of living in the United States? This was, initially, something of a stumper. Our national stats when compared worldwide weren't looking as good. We mentioned one tangible: taxes which were significantly less painful on the whole next to France (where all that state funding came from).

But other positives were harder to quantify. Yann touched on a sense of charity and volunteerism that was not present in Europe. He told one story of his experience participating in the Pan-Massachusetts challenge, a cycling event that raises money for cancer research, and sending out, prior to the event, an email to friends soliciting sponsorship. Of the donations he received, none of them were from the French contingent of his email group. The idea is more peculiar to the French who have long relied on the state to take care of its citizens' needs. The impulse to become personally involved, or to come together voluntarily for a common purpose, isn't as strong in France.

He dovetailed this with stories of the differing work ethics. He pointed out that Americans are more likely to understand the stake they have in their employer's success and regard having a job as a privilege they need to work to keep. In France, a job is often viewed as something that every citizen is owed.

I then wondered aloud when was the last time a French film or a French musical act became a global sensation. Cecile always balked at this argument and responded by singing Johnny Hallyday tunes at top volume in my direction. But since Johnny Hallyday is maybe the only longstanding, bonafide rock n' roll star France has to offer, since he lifted his entire act from American rock stars of the fifties and has continued the image through to his recent "Route 66" tour, since he splits his time between Los Angeles and Switzerland to skirt French tax laws, Cecile's singing example tends to prove my point.

Our America vs. France scorecard, by now, was too messy to be tallied and very much incomplete. Among the four of us sitting around Yann and Sophie's dinner table, all small girls tucked into bed, we didn't have anything resembling a workable conclusion about which nation holds a better life for us.

Of course, we never will. Both of our households will be forever in search of the best mix, *le bon mélange*, with the hope that maybe our daughters can take the cultural blend they were born into and shape it into something greater than its two imperfect halves.

- - -

We needed provisions. This was something America was happy to provide and at whatever hour of the day we might choose. I suggested we get up at 2 AM to get to the supermarket; just to get a glimpse of the illuminated Open 24 hours sign with a cashier still sitting beside the register waiting for commerce to continue. I wanted to prove such fantastical visions still existed.

But instead of the wee hours, we entered the supermarket on a weekday morning along with the diligent parade of seniors, stay-at-home moms and oddballs operating outside the 9 to 5 work week. The standard supermarket chain looked the same as I'd remembered from days shopping as a bachelor or, back much further, tagging along with my own mother. But as we stepped further inside, past the beach balls and value packs of Oreos both on sale up front, it became apparent that this would grow into a foreign and near-incomprehensible experience. I was lost in a land of exotic culinary marvels and forgot entirely that I was once, or still continued somehow to be, an American consumer.

Louise took up her usual place in our shopping cart's pull-out seat, the same as in France except that this one had a warning to customers not to fold the seat back down without first removing the child. An absurd vision flashed in my mind of the parent who'd filed the suit to warrant such a reminder.

The seat was baffling, like much of the contents of the store. We'd come from the land where cheese can give off odors that are nearly visible to the naked eye, quail gets stewed in its juice with cognac and where lobster is eaten at Christmas. All this tends to obscure how lovely a simple chip can be. Magically, the chip was the first item that presented itself to us under the bright lights of aisle 1. Chips and snacks, it turned out, received two full dedicated aisles and customers were required to pass munchies first in order to access the rest of the store.

We sighted nachos and pretzels, popcorns of all glazes and microwavable servings, iridescent cheese curls, puffs, three-dimensional crisps, and the vast innovations in the area of potato chips. Items had a hint of lime, were blasted with cheese or offered schizoid flavor combinations like pizza and chipotle ranch mixed together in the same bag. All of them without exception had at least one derivative of corn as an ingredient, even if only high-fructose corn syrup, the unseen but omnipresent tribute to federal corn subsidies by now as traditional as apple pie.

Other offerings were naturally baked and had real-life ingredients, which the packaging proclaimed as a revelation. In these cases, healthy eating had morphed with snacking. Kid's snacks had taken full advantage of health-conscious parents and sold crackers with the vegetable flavors that adults couldn't be expected to swallow such as spinach or kale.

On the shelves opposite the snacks were the beverages (non-alcoholic that is, as the booze needed to be cordoned off in another section altogether, the porno mags of the beverage world). Here the liquid choices were just as breathtaking. Iced tea had flavors whose taste I couldn't guess like cloudberry or yumberry pomegranate. On the adjacent shelf were the energy drinks, shot through with caffeine, vitamins and performance and mood-enhancing supplements that soon gave the aisle the look of a mini-pharmacy.

Julie and Louise had skipped ahead. I heard them squealing one aisle over about cartoon characters they knew on boxes. When they brought the package to me, I too recognized the Disney fish Nemo and Dory, but I had forgotten completely what a fruit gusher was. A candy maybe, or an actual fruit product? Raisins, peut-être? Again, the flavor told me nothing – G Force Tropical Rage. The girls capitalized on my confusion by helping themselves to a box each and paraded around the store with them like trophies. The fruit gushers had been stacked beside a host of other products from the world of little tyke cuisine, where the big draw was that everything was lunchable or chewable. Cecile had meanwhile gotten stuck on the juice box varieties, and, in the end, asked for my help in hoisting a Value Pack of Juicy Juice into our cart. With the vegetable puffies and the straws on the boxes, my girls would barely need to use their hands at all to eat a purportedly balanced meal.

We proceeded to the granola and the breakfast cereals which I remembered how much I missed, as French culture never thought much of breakfast beyond croissants and coffee. I also came across pancake mix and syrup and then enormous loaves of sliced bread. The French categorize sliced loaves of bread as a something else altogether, since a baguette is a daily purchase. White slices in plastic bags are labeled "American bread," suggesting it's not bread at all. In the New World, the corner bakery is a rare specialty shop, so the wide varieties of sliced bread, from oat bran to seven grain and then branching out to pita and tortilla wraps, surprised me. I took the liberty of adding multiple bags as a taste test.

On the far end, the aisles opened into the produce section. Whereas the snack foods came in endless taste options, the fruit and vegetables on display came in basics. The food was fresh, though the bananas looked altered to be more spotless and of a deeper yellow. Over in the meat department, the packaged steaks looked pink and watery compared to the rich reds you get at a French butcher. More appetizing were multiple brands of beef jerky hanging in pouches from shelves throughout the store. I found myself tempted by the grass-fed, hickory-smoked gourmet jerky dangling at eye level from the tissue and toilet paper area.

But in keeping with paradox, an abundance of food on display was desperate to announce its organicness. There were also more independent enterprises; the microbreweries alone far outnumbered the giant distilleries. Great porter ale made just up the street crowded out the Budweiser. Again, I felt the need to toss this onto our heap.

The last item I picked up on the way out was a jar of peanut butter. "For peanut butter and jelly sandwiches, you know, quick lunches," I told Cecile.

"What kind of sandwiches, exactly?" she asked worried. She never considered the peanut butter and jelly sandwich, in any way, a meal. For her, it was possibly a dessert or maybe something one feeds to pet hamsters. She was right that the sugar content in peanut butter, taken by itself, rivals most candy bars. Combine it with jelly and the sandwich is essentially no different in sweetness than a piece of birthday cake. But if you're going to start impugning PB & J to Americans, you might as well use the stars and stripes to towel off after using a bidet. Peanut butter and jelly is such a staple of our youthful diet that no one wants to ponder that it might be bad for the body. I ate a peanut butter and jelly sandwich for lunch nearly every weekday of my life from age six to age fifteen. Was this malnutrition? Probably. I added a single jar of Jif to the cart.

We left the supermarket that day with a teetering mountain in our shopping cart and not enough cabinet or fridge space in our rented camper van to contain all the resplendent items. I choose to meet this excess head-on by doubling down. The way to solve too much was to add just a bit more. So I decided to stop at another long pined-for dream factory: Dunkin Donuts.

This fabled donut shop was at the far end of the same parking lot. Nonetheless, we drove there. Inside, the powdered sugar smell that seemed coated onto the walls and tabletops let me know I'd come to the right place. I got an assortment box and we sat down at a booth to dig in. It was the first time my daughters had ever eaten a donut.

Before I opened the pink box of dozen that I held in my hands like a treasure chest, I looked around the shop. The atmosphere of Dunkin Donuts had changed. The design had been revamped since I'd last darkened one of these doors, possibly more than ten years ago. The donut shop was now something more sleek and sporty. The new logo slapped on every available surface looked like it belonged to a running shoe company and the colors inside suggested a business that was trying to look upscale and Web 2.0. Signs made reference to the DD Difference. I also noticed new menu items. I could order hash browns or cookies or maybe complement my donuts with a toasted flatbread sandwich. The beloved establishment with its foolproof formula of donuts and coffee was suffering from an identity crisis.

Maybe I was expecting a wee bit much from a nationwide chain, but the Dunkin Donuts I used to frequent on a Friday night after a high school football game or on Sunday mornings before my parents shuffled my siblings and me into church felt like a place where the customers completed the picture, where we were a part of the milieu. Now, I felt like a user on the receiving end of a strategy.

Cecile, meanwhile, was skeptical of the gluttony all over. I tried to emphasize the fun of it - an exception, just this once. But my side of the argument was hopelessly flimsy. It is a position I find myself in more than I wish living outside American cultural norms in general and trying to prove any of its merits to my family in particular.

Many things quintessential to my way of life have by now been well-proven to be bad for your mental or physical health. Nonetheless, agreeing with the detractors, specifically when outside of my country missing the warm and inviting atmosphere of a Dunkin Donuts, I feel like a murderous traitor. To non-Americans, most often to my wife, I would praise donuts, while I'd turn to the girls and remind them this was terrible junk food.

After more donuts than I took time to count, I stood from the table with an oddly emboldened feeling like I'd just eaten several swatches of home insulation. With it, a soporific flush hit my head that dulled clarity and, at once, removed a measure of apprehension. We'd head south or maybe west first. I was pretty sure. Either way, we would be fine. I got behind the wheel of our equally stuffed vehicle and pushed off, ballooning away from the shopping center.

Still the donuts had been, as always and despite their marketing teams best efforts to ignore them, heavenly. They convinced me I still belonged in these parts. I could power to the California redwoods with this knowledge.

We said goodbye to our first hosts and headed back the way we came. I was disappointed to be retracing our path over the same stretch of road, but this was the most direct way to Pennsylvania, where we had loved ones waiting.

Only three days into it, we'd also already changed the schedule. In the interest of spontaneity I'd replied to Cecile "why not" when she suggested we stay on another night in Massachusetts. We were enjoying the time with these friends. We could still stick to a loose calendar. But as it turns out, there's really no such thing as partial spontaneity. Changing plans for one night bumped up the arrival day at my parents' and grandmother's and, down the road, gave us less time to show up to our first campsite on the reserved day. So I figured we could make up the day with a mammoth stretch of driving, going from Reading, Mass to Lancaster, PA in one haul, over eight hours according to most estimates.

Packing our things up back at the friends' house, I tried to pretend that I wasn't hurrying to leave. But I failed to fool even Louise. An irritated exchange erupted between Cecile and me as I carried things into the camper over exactly what we were trying to do with this vacation, a renewed version of the daily planner-wielding taskmaster vs. the thrower of caution to the wind. We'd need to iron out the dispute on the road.

Cecile and I were in for an entire summer where we'd rarely be more than ten feet apart. Each day would unveil a fresh batch of choices we'd need to agree on. But there was a welcome side effect. Disagreements were often settled by, very literally, moving on. We would leave the physical destination behind where a dispute had kicked up and set out for new surroundings, which provided enough distractions and new sets of decisions to sideline the argument until the next stop where we'd forget what it was we were so cranky about.

We made it to the Hudson River Valley again before actually talking. I asked, "So, still mad?"

"Yes...and you?"

"Yes. But now I that I think about it, I expected you to be madder the day we picked up the camper."

"Why?"

"Because I chose a bad rental agency."

"Oh that I didn't care about. I was too excited that day."

"You are a recurring unsolved mystery."

"Hey, what is a Cracker Barrel?" Cecile changed the subject and tone, as we passed a billboard advertising the restaurant miles ahead.

"It's a place with starchy country cooking slathered with kitschy Americana."

"It is almost lunchtime, isn't it?"

"We should probably stop there."

"I think this is an excellent idea."

"Really? From the person who didn't like Dunkin Donuts?"

"We all have sacrifices to make."

"Okay, but once we get to Pennsylvania, we have to stop planning the trip around food."

SAVE FOR FIREFLIES

- - -

Allow me to present the state of Pennsylvania. This is your mid-Atlantic workhorse of a commonwealth, your connector of the Northeast to the rest of the country. This is a state so central to American geography and history that the rest of the country barely remembers it's there, like oxygen or window caulking. I, meanwhile, have trouble forgetting. If I had a state to call home, it would be this Keystone.

As we veered south, years started to dissolve as I got closer to Lancaster and York counties. The dark green rolling hills I remembered came into view. The roads became potholed. The houses looked more obsessed with austere red brick, their yards more populated by deer statues and portly garden gnomes. The Turkey Hill Minit Markets became more frequent, displaying the outdated logo of the profile of an American Indian.

These were the communities I'd used as my reference point for the dozens of others I'd lived in since, where I passed my adolescence burning to leave as soon as possible and then, once I had, wished from overseas that I could get back.

So I slowed down in the right lane. I passed shiny-topped silos poking up over the hills of light brown soil and deep green crops, hand-painted signs for sweet corn and the names on the highway panels like Ephrata, New Holland and the Amish communities infamously called Virginville, Blue Ball and Intercourse. Our family had debated more than once whether the Amish had chosen those names out of obliviousness to their connotations or if this was an indication of some suppressed ribald humor. I liked to assume the latter.

I flipped on the local radio station, 98.5 FM, the frequency responsible for providing a soundtrack to my teenage years. The song currently playing was something from Pearl Jam, released over fifteen years ago. A slightly less dated Smashmouth hit followed this. This station hadn't changed its rotation in more than ten years. The new generation of teenage listeners had satellite radio connected to their iPods while, meanwhile, the radio airwaves of central PA had hardly budged.

My parents even had moved on. Since the emptying of their nest, they'd left the house where I grew up in York for a smaller place in downtown Lancaster, the rival town just over the Susquehanna River. I didn't know my way around this city and there was no single room of the house there that previously belonged to me.

Why then, did I enter my parents house and instantly recognize the dimpled dark blue drinking glasses set out when guests came or the N.C. Wyeth painting of children on a beach peering up at a giant in the clouds that I'd once mistaken for a photograph? And speaking of photographs, who were those three children in front of the powder-blue Olan Mills backdrop in braces and 1980s-style clothing? Why did I get the sense, these things before my eyes, of not going about life as the sole person responsible for my own well being? It wasn't home, but I still had the recurring impression that it might be close. I felt watched over again.

An added comfort returned to my bones, as it always did upon returning to my parents. It has always induced in me more clownish and impulsive behavior. It has always rolled me back to age eighteen.

Just as soon as the regression settled in, my girls scurried past my knees and into the house. Before I acted upon my reflex to raid my parents' fridge, like I'd just gotten back from after-school tennis practice, I noticed my mom and dad blowing bubbles off the back porch to peals of girlish laughter. For a half-second the thought occurred, "I have daughters?" Cecile talked with my mom about clothes for them. "And a wife!" I thought, "Wow, you lucky bastard!"

The fountain of youth illusion that my parents' household held, no matter the house, vanished. Age eighteen, lest I forget, had its limitations. In its place, the awareness of my own growth during these early years of adulthood rang in my head like a gong.

It also happened to be Father's Day. The occasion didn't involve any cards or presents or grand celebrations but rather new mutual well-wishing between my own father and me. After the fun with the bubbles, he and I stood in the kitchen doorway and nodded, "Happy Father's Day to you!" "No, to you." "No, you." It became comical, as Dads tend to inherently be. Though my Dad is funnier. He will also always be well beyond me in understanding the essential reflection of fatherly grace comes in stepping out of the way when the family is simply happy to be whole together.

My mom led us into the garage to show us the items she'd been storing for us purchased online weeks ahead of time. She was almost as keyed up about our travels as we were, so much so that they'd be joining us on a portion of it out west in a month. But for now, as we took our own inventory, she wanted to hear about the destinations that lay ahead for us.

After I ran through our plans, she noted, "It's going to be interesting to see what you think of the country. My guess is that you'll see things have changed."

"What do you mean?"

"Well, a lot of people are worried. You'll see. Things aren't quite the same. People's moods are terrible. Everything - oh it's hard to say - it's just kind of down."

The first half of the year 2008 had been a nervous one for the country. Unemployment spiked at the same rate as gas prices. Two wars had devolved quickly into catastrophes. Extreme weather patterns had more of the population questioning if it was possible that we'd done irreparable damage to the natural world around us.

I tended to be an optimist. But when your mother says a lot of people are worried and describes the overall mood around her as down, you tend to take it as gospel truth, despite what you might attempt to dismiss as an unfounded maternal anxiety for her adult children out somewhere beyond her safekeeping. In your heart though, you still adopt a part of this outlook as reality. When something is wrong, I have the urge to set out to do something about it, beginning with trying to cheer up my mother.

"I don't know, Mom, the predictions of America's downfall feel exaggerated to me. But what do I know, I'm just a tourist."

"Well, you'll probably see a little bit of everything."

"How are things at work?"

"Oh, for me it's the usual." She went on to explain working with a new dean at the college where she'd been for the past ten years.

"It's your Dad though. We'll just have to see how working from home suits him."

My Dad's company, a textbook graphics outfit, had recently downsized. They'd closed their offices in central PA and laid off half of the employees. Those who were fortunate enough to keep their jobs, like my Dad, were asked to telecommute, working from home each day, with occasional visits to the main offices in New Jersey. It seemed like a lucky break for him. He was positive about the change. He wouldn't have to fight traffic anymore.

"But, Dad's position is not in danger, is it?" I asked.

"No, no, he should be secure now," my Mom said reassuring all of us, including herself. But one other thing I wanted to ask before I forget, do you have enough warm blankets?"

"Mom, you don't need to," I immediately rejected the idea that we needed anything, quick to brandish my autonomy for her benefit. Then, I actually listened. "Now that you mention it, we don't have many blankets."

"That's what I thought…"

Essential Road and Camping Items
* sheets and blankets
* huge blue tarp
* canvas folding camping chairs
* water shoes for the girls
* maps and atlases
* French press coffee mug
* tick remover key
* snake bite kit
* hand axe
* bungee cords
* duct tape
* value pack of all-purpose utility wipes
* dustpan and brush
* citronella candle
* insect repellent
* clip-on reading lamp
* screened-in lantern to hold captured insects with butterfly net
* Camp Out! The Ultimate Kids Guide to Camping by Lynn Brunelle
* D.W. The Picky Eater by Marc Brown
* Curious George Dreams by H.A. Rey

Items Purchased I Assumed Were Essential But Would Go Unused
* bear spray
* binoculars
* clothespins and clothesline

* teapot (while camping it really mattered not if the water was heated in a saucepan)
* tire pressure gauge (the PSI for our camper's tires went beyond the max 80 that most gauges feature)
* travel neck pillows for the girls (instantly deemed uncomfortable by the users)
* sporks
* campfire waffle iron

In my parents' driveway, Cecile arranged the camper while I stood by the open door asking questions and making smart remarks. Emphasis on the smart remarks. My lack of any assistance wasn't intentional. Cecile had barred me from any and all making of house.

In Dijon, we'd established a workable arrangement of non-traditional parenting roles. I took care of the girls and the home front during the day, keeping time on the side for writing, while Cecile worked full time, commuting into Paris by train where she was rising in the ranks of management at the Paris bureau of her PR agency. It suited our individual personalities, she thrived on the mile-a-minute people-pleasing skills required for her work and I was good at the quieter, forever unfinished battles at home that meshed with a newcomer to the surrounding language and country. Home was my own domain. Work satisfied Cecile's longtime ambitions. We were comfortable in the roles and both equally proud of the other.

But in the states, our roles tilted conventional somehow. I was the one who drove the camper and lorded over the map and itinerary, and Cecile tended to the kids and cooked and cleaned. Was it because I was more at ease as a characteristic father in my own country? Was it also perhaps that we still needed to gratify some of these assigned gender roles still hard-wired into our DNA? In the camper that afternoon before shoving on again, Cecile hummed contentedly as she folded clothes into the drawer. I studied, without any sense of redundancy, the map.

"You know, Louise, will refuse to wear those socks." I pointed out, the stay-at-home parent once again.

"I'll think she'll like them," Cecile replied.

"We'll see about that. And also where's the other piece to this bathing suit of Julie's?" I held up the bottom half of a pink and purple bikini.

"She just has the bottom. She doesn't need the top."

"Except we're in the U.S. of A. now."

"She's four years old, who cares!"

"I don't, but the people on the beaches and public pools of this country do."

"I find this stupid."

"Me too. But around here, whatever the age, a topless girl is a topless girl. People will notice and there's no reason to have her push the envelope."

"You're being too self-conscious," Cecile responded. She'd arrived at the truth of the matter. I cared more what people thought in my home country. In France, I was already strange by virtue of my accent, my occasional baseball cap and the way I flubbed the cheek-kiss greetings. I soon ceased to care if anything else I did or said was also strange or off-putting. In numerous instances in Dijon, Cecile advised me on what to say or do because of how it looked to strangers in the street, to whom I was either oblivious or willfully dismissive. Justified or not, she felt she had to live up to a kind of standard.

In America, I became concerned about the regard of others, while Cecile let things go. After all, no one would likely say a word about a little girl's lack of top. Still, I now cared again.

We were sifting through the patterns of behavior, built around gender and culture that we'd be keeping or tossing to the side of the road. I clung to the hope that the motion would illuminate whatever we couldn't yet make sense of.

We traveled west across the Susquehanna River in central Pennsylvania, entering the county and then city of York. York is an average, mid-sized city among the dark green hills of the valley named after the river, but only an hour's drive north of the Baltimore-Washington churn. It is a place rich in history that lays claim to the title of the "first capital of the United States," as it held this status during the American Revolution allowing the Continental Congress to adopt the Articles of Confederation and then move the capital elsewhere.

York is a city that's seen a development explosion in its suburbs, but still maintains a downtown with a weekend market, a symphony orchestra, the offices of not one, but two, daily newspapers and a spiking crime rate. Speaking broadly, its citizens tend to be of German descent, hold conservative, hard-working Protestant values and avoid showiness where a simple nod will do.

SAVE FOR FIREFLIES

York is getting by okay. It is named for the town in England. It is the subject of the song Shit Towne by the popular 90s band Live, whose members were themselves native Yorkers.

Nationally, York is also renowned for peppermint patties, barbells and its Harley-Davidson factory. A recent branding strategy by the Chamber of Commerce bills York County as "The Factory Tour Capital of the World," though it's really only the Harley plant that's worth coming for. Other selected tours include that of a local credit union and, listed in brochures without a hint of a joke, a landfill.

Internationally, I get questions about my hometown. When I say I'm from York, I'm asked about the city's possible relation to the Big Apple.

"No, no," I clarify, "it's just York."

"This is the old York then? The original city, before the New one?" they'll ask, interest piqued.

"Almost," I nod.

I find myself rarely with the right moment to describe what the place is to me.

It's the smell of the deep green grass of our backlawn just mowed by my father and the fading light coming through the oaks above it as the fireflies rise to waist level. It's the scent of honeysuckle that wafts in. It's getting picked up by a friend later and roaming the backroads trying to come up with something to do, somewhere in this town there's got to be something. It's not being able to wait to get out for good.

York is breakfast apple butter on toast, with chipped beef gravy that could also just as easily be for lunch in which case it comes with Utz potato chips and root beer in Penn State Nittany Lion souvenir cups. If it's in my grandmother's kitchen it will be finished with shoo-fly pie, the sweetest substance known to humankind.

Of the later years, my memories are sharper, by virtue of their proximity to the leaving I needed to do so badly. York became a bar where everyone shared pitchers of Yuengling, referred to only as "Lager" and then driving all the way to the river where someone had strung a rope swing over a high branch. The night would conclude with me getting dropped off and lingering for a few seconds in the backyard before turning in, as I listened to the ratchet sound of the katydids and the high shallow chirp of the crickets coming from the darkness around me.

I'd move to California and find myself missing all of this fiercely.

Now I found York ahead of me again. I followed the exit signs to 83 South. I came back to a spot knowing I probably wouldn't see the woods in the dark. If I did run into anyone, I knew they wouldn't recognize me stepping as I would be out of a rented camper van.

I saw a new Walgreens across the street from the still newer CVS. A seafood restaurant where I'd also worked a few summers as a busboy had since changed names and ownership and then closed down entirely, standing now as a paint-chipped, lazily tagged eyesore by the highway. More tract housing pushed into open meadows and farmland. More construction sites lay quiet and half-finished, waiting for the money to flow again. More houses had "For Sale" signs in the front yard with a lending bank as the contact. But it would get worse.

Despite initial reluctance to disturb the dream, I decided to visit my old neighborhood. One of my good friends, with whom I'd spent those weekend and summer nights, had moved into a house up the street with his wife and two young boys. He stayed in York, a choice I envied at times. He'd even gotten a job teaching at our old high school. So his memories had been superseded by a busy present. His nostalgia wasn't so precious.

He appeared bigger somehow, not in weight, but in general stature. His hair had faded gray at the edges. His tone of voice had subdued. But his long-armed greeting and his sideways glancing grin hadn't changed.

Our kids played together in the yard as we caught up. He sensed we were itching to travel, as I made an attempt I knew was futile from the start, to convince him to join us part of the way. Instead, we made plans to stay longer on the return end of the trip.

I had a similar memory dissonance when I drove by my old house on the way out.

The building remained, but there was an incongruous pickup truck in the driveway, new shuttered windows, odd plants in the front yard and a decorative flag on the porch. These were minor details of the new owner's presence.

They were enough, nonetheless, to transform this house into an anonymous address I'd never laid on eyes before. I heard a voice from inside the garage. I couldn't linger any longer. Soon dusk would fall and the fireflies would rise again from the grass, followed by the sound of the insects coming out of the still haunted woods. The memory of home had to be saved from this place that was so aggressively not home. Once again, we'd need to look elsewhere.

I drove off, taking the new access road, linking our neighborhood to the highway.

Places I Might Belong
* a bassinet in Southern California
* a Lake Erie beach digging holes to China
* the house in York with the fireflies and the woodland monsters of childhood
* San Francisco
* an Iowa farm, where great-grandparents had lived and were buried
* wherever the guidebooks suggested
* whatever place would take us

We had one last night in Pennsylvania visiting my grandmother, my only surviving grandparent. We drove west of York to her retirement community not far from the Civil War battlefields of Gettysburg.

She'd recently celebrated her ninetieth birthday. I sensed that she understood, without needing to hear the details, the spirit of our trip. Her thoughts leapt westward ahead of us, to her childhood on an Iowa farm during the Depression and to the descriptions of my great-great grandparents and the family making a life there. I knew their faces only from old photographs and her stories. She spoke often of this time of her life, and as she did, I conjured aspects of these ancestors' smiles, the earnestness in the approach to daily work and the humility of common gesture that I hoped I held somewhere in my bones.

Our family sat down once more at my grandmother's table. We said grace before the meal, something which my girls and Cecile were not accustomed. Julie, for one, was calmed by the quiet holding of hands, while Louise wasn't yet ready to attempt the patience required of bowing her head while her food waited untouched in front of her.

"Louise, can you hold my hand and say this with me? It's called a prayer," I whispered.

She looked back at me puzzled, then around the table of her extended family paused, holding hands. She then shook her head as if to say "no thanks" and returned to the noodles before her.

My grandmother walked into the June sunlight to see us off in the morning. She handed an old stuffed animal she'd kept for years to each of the girls. To Cecile and me, she presented an envelope with money inside and a note that promised she'd be "watching our travels from afar."

I was struck with that same, sinking feeling I wished I could avoid: time, our own shared span of it, was moving much faster than when I'd last visited. It would continue to accelerate toward the next return to her doorstep. Though there was no guarantee I'd ever be back. It might not be long before she wouldn't be there to greet us.

This stirred up a conflicting urge to either stay the whole summer with her while we still had the chance or set out in exploration of the open-sky elsewhere waiting for us.

I knew only what she would prefer we do.

SAVE FOR FIREFLIES

SOUTH - - -

From our bedroom window in Dijon we can see the soaring Gothic steeple of the Dijon Saint Benigne Cathedral. Its spires are decorated with ornate, larger than life-sized sculptures and its roof displays the interlocking red and beige diamond patterns traditional to Burgundy architecture. In the Spring, the moon rises from behind the cathedral. Sometimes, waking in the middle of the night, I glance out expecting to see a nightwatchman snuffing out candles in the street lamps.

In the months before our trip, however, I went to bed beside the Gothic scene while reading about the hiking trails of Utah's Bryce Canyon. Other times I'd be rolling through the Burgundy countryside on an afternoon drive and I'd catch myself summoning visions of our family rounding a picket fence-lined bend along the Blue Ridge Parkway. Or I'd stroll through one of the Dijon's parks with the girls and glance up at the trees, seeing there a towering California Sequoia.

The beauty of France, in the weathered stone reminders of its history, in its muted pastoral landscape, can never be denied, but that spring it all held something less when compared to the full-tilt magnificence of the wilds of America.

And then, a week after landing on American soil, the planning and preparation unfurled into the real thing. The journey kicked in. On this highway out of Pennsylvania, our movement took on a trajectory and a pace. Maybe because I was leaving "home" once again, the United States felt enormous. It was the size of a universe all its own that erased the existence of all other places outside. From within U.S. borders, the country looked impossible to grasp as one whole, whereas from another continent I could view it from above, encapsulate it and see the lot of it. I could make broad connections. As we aimed for the mountains of Virginia, I couldn't believe this soil fanned out to the deserts of New Mexico and the forests of Oregon. Only the atlas reassured me. Otherwise, we traversed the territory of an endless undiscovered world.

The highway was as wide as a river. The camper stood high on its wheels and rocked from side to side so that loose straps and towels hung to dry in the back swayed to the road rhythm. A low shimmy and squeak came from the cabover compartment, used for fastened-down overflow storage when in motion. I switched off the air conditioner. We rolled down the windows inviting the boisterous wind. I doublechecked that the four of us were fastened down ourselves.

Would I finally be able to stop looking days and weeks ahead now that I'd entered this new sphere? Could I enjoy it for what it actually was? Because likely nothing would meet my expectations by now. Inflated and gussied up by saccharine memory, my American dream was an illusion more improbable than any awestruck immigrant's vision of the land of opportunity.

Balmy weather had followed us below the Mason Dixon line. We passed family minivans and pickup trucks, groups of Harley riders, convoys of trucks and larger RVs, and a sedan with a *McCain for President* bumper sticker and another near-identical sedan with an Obama sticker. All of them moved slower than those we'd shared the road with in the Northeast. We headed straight into the Blue Ridge Mountains, beginning at the northernmost point of Skyline Drive and then the entrance to our first national park.

Shenandoah was officially established in the 1930s, in an attempt to bring the preserved park experience to the eastern part of the country after its popularity in the West. The creation of government land in these mountains displaced hundreds of inhabitants who'd made homes here. Some too stubborn to accept leaving had been permitted to finish out their days here, the rest were pushed out. The last few residents who remained passed away in the 1970s.

Since then, the wildlife has reigned. Nature is interrupted only by the five campgrounds and two lodges and the main road through. The park has miles of trails and scenic lookouts at every curve in the road.

Daniel Boone called this area the land of many views. It was a vague summary, but after all the soaring scenic turnouts showing us what he meant, I couldn't think of a better way to describe it. The untouched forest mountains stretched to the visible horizon line. We looked beyond the stone walls that abutted the turnouts into nothing but misty green as far as we could see. All this waited only sixty miles from the D.C. beltway.

We caboosed onto a line of vehicles negotiating the Skyline. The pace cars reminded me to take my time. Within the forest trails, we spotted families carrying picnic baskets and children letting the streamers on their bikes fly. Among them, two hikers with cargo-like backpacks and layers of grime trudged against the traffic. They were AT hikers, passing through the populated portion of the 2,160-mile mythic Appalachian Trail. If they were hiking the full trail, they'd started at Springer Mountain in Georgia and wouldn't stop the northbound beat until they reached the far tip of Maine. There they would say they'd done it. Their trek had purpose not because of the destination they would reach but because of the line they would trace. The trail passed just west of York where I'd known people who considered hiking the AT as the closest thing a god-fearing Germanic Protestant had to a pilgrimage to Mecca. There was something on that fabled walk. Only after you left your bootprint along every mile marker would you understand what and could you then be granted a modicum of the respect the trail itself demanded.

We passed the trekkers going in the other direction, blazing our own separate trail. Our rhythm required less concentration, and with kids in the absence of physical sport, another kind of the sacrifice of time. Our goal was not end-to-end, just a completed loop.

Our new National Park annual pass, purchased at the ranger booth at the entrance, hung like a badge of honor out of the camper's sun visor. Cecile read over the brochure of privileges from the passenger seat, along with the inserted leaflet of lengthy instructions about camping and proper food storage that featured the word BLACK BEARS in bold letters all over the pages of the brochure. More alarmist reminders about the dangers of feeding the wildlife had been posted along the side of the road or tacked up on trees near the campground.

So I kicked up some fear of the bear to everybody. From that point on, as we continued deeper into the park, the only thought on the girls' minds was a bear sighting.

"I see one behind that tree!" Julie warned her sister. "An enormous one!"

"Oooo," Louise cooed, hoping, I guessed, to see one snacking on a hiker.

"Hey, we have a spot reserved here," Cecile said, pleasantly surprised to find herself pleasantly surprised at my advance preparation.

We were home because the name "Missildine" was clipped to one of Loop A's campsite markers at the Big Meadows campground. Still, we kept the camper facing out and left the keys in the ignition for a quick getaway if needed.

To inaugurate the camping life, a group of old college friends of mine joined us, most of whom I hadn't seen in years. They converged on our campsite soon after we arrived, coming around the bend of the campground loop, on their way back from a hike. They looked as enchanted to me as a group of woodland elves, the kind who wear sensible T-shirts and carry Nalgene water bottles. I tried to tamp down my nostalgia again.

"Ok then!" an old dorm mate and true friend announced.

"So this is your ride?" another chortled, either impressed by or aghast at the camper, I wasn't sure which.

What happens to college friends? Mine had come together at a moment when our late-blooming social openness and impulse to live deliberately and sincerely had clicked. This made for an inseparability in an environment already incubated, where we had the time to praise urgent ideas, entertain romantic neuroses and share charmed moments that made it possible to believe the future would be perfect. The whole thing was bound not to be repeated.

And it had been ten years since we'd left it. Given a starting point in such contrast to the real world, we'd all come out surprisingly well-adjusted. One friend was working for the U.S. State department. He had just recently accepted an overseas post in Cameroon, where he and his wife would spend two years as he worked for the American embassy. Another was a research physicist, then studying the neurological pathways of rats. Yet another had spent the past year as a speechwriter for the presidential campaign of Hillary Clinton. As of June 2008, the grueling Democratic primary just finished, this guy was currently looking for employment. Still another friend was, like me, a writer trying to carve out a career. She'd also married the physicist.

So among these roads taken I wasn't sure how adjusted I was. Mine was its own unforeseen meander and, among this particular group at this point in our lives, the only one that included children. I was the family man. Being both the Dad and the ex-pat, I felt a little out of step with the easy guffaws and snappy observations that once marked our collegiate days and nights. As we launched into catching up, I wasn't sure if I was still allowed to act like the happy jackass I was in college. Did a wife and two children thrown into the picture douse the spark?

As we caught up, I grew less certain, not more. My humor, usually a meaningful kind of communication with this group, seemed canned and irrelevant. I started talking and asking questions and felt the vast uncovered remainder that the current conversation was only touching upon. Without the fresh exuberance that accompanied us in our early days, we may never be brought back to experiencing things from a shared perspective. Meanwhile, my attention was divided between them and the girls. Should I really be listening to my friend tell me about a Youtube video while Julie broke into the bag of marshmallows before her dinner? Was I being fair to either party?

A storm kicked up and we all huddled in the camper to wait it out. We set up a makeshift addition to our camper with a tarp and the open back door. My concerns fell away, precisely why I'd enjoyed the company of these people in the first place. In whatever kind of future it had turned out to be, no one here was interested in whether I was making an impression.

One friend turned to me: "So, Nat, you'll be living out of this thing for three months? Basically, you've gone insane."

I proceeded to press him for dirt on Hillary Clinton. He only insisted that Barack Obama turned out to be too brilliant a politician.

"Do you think he can win in November?"

"He better," came his immediate response.

Once the rain let up, we managed a fire and hot dogs and roasted corn-on-the-cob in aluminum foil as the mountains grew cold and people began draping themselves in blankets. From there, talk turned to music and movies, other friends not in attendance and other things that all made us feel older.

Julie and Louise both went to sleep without complaint (a lucky first that wouldn't always be repeated). Among the group at this campsite they felt well-protected and among family. In any case, they could tell this was their father's sense of the evening. I'd like to think they were following my lead.

Not long after the girls, everyone else turned in for the night. They all had to get back. We, on the other hand, had to get away some more.

According to a study conducted by the National Academy of Sciences visits to national parks have steadily declined since a peak in 1987. The study attributed this directly to the rise in videogame and Internet usage.

But I wasn't convinced. The Big Meadows campground was nearly full on a Sunday night. The visitors we encountered walked around in a state close to awe and most seemed to be working hard to leave the smallest possible trace. Added to that, the nature here still dominated, making the campers, whatever their numbers, look insignificant. The wildlife presence still dominated.

We would never see any bears. Shenandoah made up for this absence with whitetail deer. These creatures passed through our campsite on such a consistent basis that we began to wonder if we were situated on some kind of migratory thoroughfare. The girls, meanwhile, were stunned the first time a deer appeared grazing within feet of our site's picnic table. The animals might as well have been giraffes. The girls grew comfortable, thanks to the frequent sightings, and took to chasing them. I explained to Julie that she wouldn't be able catch one, which she took as a kind of dare. Louise followed her sister's lead. They skipped into the overgrowth far behind the distant leaping deer.

Then Louise fell, just beyond the campsite boundary. Cecile and I winced at the sight of her tumbling into the dirt and brush. We rushed to her.

Louise rolled over to reveal a cut opening on her forehead. She called out "Daddy!" through her tears, but Cecile cradled in her arms first. She moved our whimpering daughter to the picnic table to look at the wound. After the shock had passed, Louise still wanted a hug from me. Cecile pulled out a band-aid featuring a cartoon ladybug, which was enough to convince Louise she'd received ICU treatment. Strapped into the cocoon of her car seat, she sighed my name a few more times for good measure.

Four hours and half of Virginia later, at the Hungry Mother State Park near the North Carolina border, we swam in a cool mountain lake. There, we found a tick embedded on the back of Julie's leg. The miniscule fiend might have been feasting on her since breakfast. We removed the insect with the tick removal key, a flat piece of metal with an oblong hole in the center that I was glad to have in my pocket. I tossed the tick into the sand and I scanned the horizon for more bad omens.

I was sort of hoping we wouldn't be this accident-prone this early on in the trip. I tried not to let my mind race over the dangers in store. Peril lay like a crouched velociraptor. I didn't know how real to make it out to be. But I worried enough to tell myself this surely would only be the beginning.

I'd read at a pit stop about the legend that gave Hungry Mother State Park its name. A woman named Molly Marley and her small daughter were captured as Native Americans, in this case likely Cherokee, destroyed settlements in the area. Eventually, they escaped and fled into the woods. The mother and daughter survived on berries until Molly finally collapsed, unable to take another step. Her daughter, however, continued on, walking along the creek until she found help. The only words she was able to utter to the occupants of the first house she came to were "Hungry. Mother."

At our campsite over dinner, with Julie de-ticked and Louise with bandaged anew, I looked up into the darkening forest and tried to imagine one of my own girls walking blindly through its brush and brambles. A tick or a bump on the head was, and from now on, a deep blessing. May it stay that way and the nastier peril let us be.

But while this father wrings his hands over the physical dangers, this mother frets over the emotional ones. Cecile hadn't moved on from the earlier incident with Louise, not because of the cut but because of Louise's impulse to call for me, instead of her. Cecile sat down beside me on the canvas camping chair in the dark, nursing her own little wound.

I could see the lights from the distant campground bathrooms and the lanterns from the campers at the adjacent site reflected in her misted-up eyes. Louise not reaching first for her mother made Cecile feel unneeded and unnecessary, like the emotionally-disconnected working parent. Who was she if she wasn't the one to console her daughter? Was she doing some kind of harm to her children by not being there all the time for them? Should she stop working and switch roles with me? Were the traditional gender roles better? The guilt gushed out of Cecile like her daughter's tears.

"Listen. No." I stopped her. "You were the first one to pick her up to make her feel better."

"She still called your name before mine."

"You're the best mother in the world for them."

"She's not used to me being there for her."

"Not true."

"I need the time with them."

"If it's your job you're talking about, you should quit. We can work something out. There are always other possibilities."

"Like what?"

"I've always wanted to break into the world of professional street mimes for instance."

"You'd make a good mime," she lightened up with me. Though it was a non-answer I gave her, it stopped the overflowing doubt.

Non-traditional parenting roles are messy. Cecile makes the big decisions about home décor and is more on top of the kids' health and doctor visits. I also spend evenings writing and teach English on the side. I never really mastered the art of ironing or braiding hair, both of which Cecile is called in for. We retain typically male and female traits, which is why I work every day to keep our place looking clean and decent and make the meals and dry the tears, but will never pass any amount of time reading a home decoration magazine. It is also why Cecile has an untiring drive to succeed in the world of business, but also will always need to cultivate an intimate maternal bond with her kids.

At those moments when the strength of that bond is called into question, such as when Louise reaches for her Dad after a bump on the head, Cecile takes it personally and feels like an outsider. Just as I absorb personally the statement that men are not capable of or meant to act as the stay-at-home parent. We'd been raising children with this successful system for almost five years, but ran into moments of second-guessing.

"You'd be ready to go back to working full-time?" Cecile asked me, serious again.

"If you're ready to be at home with the kids all day." I could see the silhouette of her head tilt in another pang of doubt over this option.

"I might go wacko."

"How about we try nine more weeks in a mobile home first?"

"That's a good start."

"Excuse me," our conversation was interrupted by a voice in the woods. An older woman with short hair and a fleece held up a soft lantern, her fellow camper another woman the same age, walked beside her. "What language were those two darlings of yours speaking?" she smiled, "We'd been wondering ourselves."

I explained where we were from.

"Is that right? The things you find in backwoods Virginia," she replied laughing.

We talked about our individual trips. These women were Southerners headed north, coming from the suburbs of Atlanta going to New York state. They had just visited the city of Asheville, North Carolina. I told her we planned to get there by the afternoon and she replied "Oh, you'll love it down there, it's very bohemian."

We were pegged as bohemian. It was perhaps the Frenchness or the fact that I counted the swim in the Hungry Mother lake as my first shower in days.

More to the point, hers was only the latest in a long line of recommendations. Asheville was the city that of late had become the darling of American travel guides, a place that countless people I knew up and down the eastern seaboard were trying to get to, bohemian or not. A friend had recently moved to Asheville from Ohio and said she didn't know why she hadn't lived there sooner. Even my parents were toying with the idea of retiring to this western North Carolina mountain paradise.

We'd be going to meet my sister, who had just recently landed a gig with the Asheville Symphony as a viola player. She too had nothing but positive reports about the place. So, we wanted to see her, but I also wanted to find out what all the fuss was about Asheville.

The next morning we crossed into North Carolina, following the Blue Ridge Mountains, and exited off the highway at Asheville's Grove Arcade market, at the center of the city's downtown. We proceeded to find both the bohemian - streetside jugglers and entertainers, boutiques selling blown glass and hand-crafted wind chimes, new age bookstores and good used CD stores with walls covered in band stickers – along with old-fashioned Southern charm – the Mast General Store selling candies in old oak barrels and the Woolworth Walk Soda Fountain serving malts and lime rickeys.

Things were also kid friendly. One bookstore had pillows provided for kids to lounge on while reading, without the huffy looks from clerks because we weren't purchasing anything, a routine occurrence in France.

We sat down in a public square to watch an outdoor hula-hooping marathon. A range of participants, young and old, some dressed in colorful pajama-like rags and some in branded workout clothes, hula-hooped together to DJ trance music. It was just the kind of loopy, community-driven event I expected. A twinge of skepticism welled up that wanted to call these people self-consciously iconoclast or just overprivileged, until I looked over at Julie mesmerized and dancing to their beat. It occurred to me that she had never seen this kind of impromptu demonstration of adults at play. She pleaded to stay long after the rest of us had lost interest.

Asheville, whether it was described as hippy or crunchy or freaky, wasn't afraid to see the world through a child's eyes. The people gathered for something creative and collective, not to compete nor even to have a particular point to make. Plus, a lot them could do impressive things with the hoop. One woman managed to keep two hoops spinning at both her waist and neck.

Still my skepticism hadn't evaporated. A few fellow spectators watching nursed bottles in brown bags. A hooded teenager circled the area muttering "smoke." A woman offered tips on making your own hula hoop, digressing into why a homemade one was better than those on sale at large superstores owned by- and here I almost completed the sentence for her- "evil multi-national corporations."

"I can picture us living in Asheville," Cecile said later that evening at the glorious Mela Indian Restaurant. I was too busy with a plate of samosa chat topped with chick peas, mint and red pepper chutney to meet this statement with the surprise it deserved, while Julie and Louise ate naan bread and drew crayon figures on the paper placemats. Out the window, guys with tattoos and girls with tube tops and baggy jeans streamed toward the city center for a concert on that summer Saturday night. An opening band somewhere warmed up a crowd.

I didn't know how serious to take Cecile when she told me she saw a life here, or if I felt the same. Asheville's nickname was the Paris of the South. I understood what this name was trying to get at, but the place swung fairly wide of any Parisian sensibility. Asheville was a place for searchers. Paris, on the other hand, was the place that had already found itself long ago, and faced the challenge of carrying its treasures into a new century. If Cecile and I were truly both considering a new place to live, we'd need something for both searchers and homebodies, American and European, New and wise Old World.

As we stepped back onto the street, a young woman passed by us twirling her hula hoop in an endless, perfect circle around her arm as she followed the throng in the direction of the distant drums. Briefly, I wanted to join them. Very briefly.

We'd follow instead other sounds farther out of town. We arrived at the campus of the Brevard Music Center after nightfall. This summer music festival and training program was tucked deeper into the western Carolina mountains. Brevard hosted students and performers for the two-month retreat. One of the students happened to be my younger sister, Nina, there to hone her skills on the viola. We'd met up with Nina back in Asheville, another familiar, smiling face in this unfamiliar country, and she led us down the road south, deeper into the mountains.

Upon arrival, the woods of the music center's campus were silent and still. But in the light of the cabin windows, we could see the silhouettes of musicians hunched over instruments and the faint sound of the scales they practiced. By the amphitheater, the stage crew was adjusting rigging in the ceiling in preparation for a weekend performance with cellist Yo-Yo Ma.

We'd be living in the institute's parking lot for two days, like traveling orchestra groupies. We selected a reasonably inconspicuous spot and turned off the camper. The chirping of crickets replaced the sound of our engine. The trill of a clarinet in the distance rose over them.

We sat down on the parking lot curb and caught up with Nina. Since the hour had grown late we started changing the girls into pajamas. But soon, out of the darkness, friends and fellow students emerged, cranking up for their own impromptu Saturday reconnect. Two former Brevard students among them were passing through like us, on a motorcycle trip to Portland, Oregon. They stepped into the gown of light hanging from the parking lot's security light and cracked open beer bottles.

But Nina shushed the group, keeping her nieces in mind. Inside the camper, both Julie and Louise were fast asleep, having drifted off on the drive back from Asheville. Cecile and I transferred them, floppy arms and tiny snores, from their car seats to the beds. It was almost seamless. Then, Louise's eyes flicked open.

"Hot." Louise murmured. "Hot, papa."

Limited vocabulary makes it easier to get to the point. Louise was right. Though, the evening was cool in this part of North Carolina, the cabover compartment of the camper that held their bed had trapped in the same humid air from midday. The camper's house air-conditioning unit didn't work unless plugged directly into a power source, so we relied on a scarcely-felt cross breeze through the camper's small overhead windows.

Julie followed Louise, throwing off the covers and rising to a seated position, her hair matted to the side of her forehead. We opened all the windows that had screens, rubbed the girls down with a cool washcloth and tried to settle them again with some bedtime reading.

But they'd found a second wind. We cooed lullabies, Frère Jacques and She'll Be Coming 'Round the Mountain in turn. But it was no use. They'd taken the quick nap and were ready for some kind of all-nighter. Since, we weren't going to throw them in with the beer-swilling group, we reemphasized the need to get to sleep for the night. We intoned an emphatic goodnight and waited just outside the camper, hoping weakly that the sounds of giggling and scratching at the screens like trapped kittens would subside. Cecile and I returned to quell their rebellion again and again, each go around with sterner reiterations over how far beyond bedtime they'd gone. Nina, having helpfully relegated the party to the nearby picnic table, stood outside the camper almost holding a straight face. She had the same thought as I did- my brother and I doing exactly the same during nights in hotels traveling as kids.

Around ten, the girls gave up the struggle. We returned to the revelers, within earshot of the girls but not too close that the revelry wouldn't have to be done in a whisper.

More six packs had appeared. Nina and her fellow students unwound those seven-hour stretches of scales and counting in sheet music measures into a nighttime energy that was bound to go well past my own regular bedtime.

Her friends were typical early twenty-somethings. Among them, I realized that the one thing missing from the night with my college friends back in Shenandoah was a sense of urgency. This evening had already taken off like a runaway train. These were the nights of their lives.

"This guy is crossing the country in an RV with his family and these two are on motorcycles? I don't know whose rolling deeper."

"I just got off the phone with my girlfriend back in Maryland. She keeps telling me the distance is gonna kill us."

"You're comparing two different things, it's like Brahms to Shostakovich."

"You know Obama still blazes the weed. I mean, c'mon!!"

"Shit, those guys with the flashlights over there, that's campus security!"

"Of course, that's why he won the North Carolina primary."

"Or else it's Yo Yo Ma."

"Screw those guys! We're not doing anything wrong."

"That's what I keep trying to tell her, if we just give ourselves some space for a year."

"We've gotta go do something, like climb the roof of the amphitheater and light off some roman candles or somethin'"

"Nah, he can't win a general election."

"I'm gonna call her again."

"Who's going for a swim down by the lake with me!"

"Dude, there're snakes in that water!"

I wondered where to enter in on these exchanges. Then I heard:

"Nat, can you go check on the girls?"

Up the next morning earlier than hoped, we ate breakfast on the same picnic table. The remnants of the evening had been crushed and stuffed into an overflowing trashcan near the amphitheater. The clarinet player now rehearsed on the stage.

The girls made sure Cecile, Nina and I didn't drag our feet that morning. After an extra trip for more coffee, we drove to Sliding Rock Recreation Area near the Pisgah National Forest, only a few miles from the music school.

The woods provided a refuge. The staggered bends of the stream at Sliding Rock create a Blue Ridge waterfall with shallow pools between larger, dry rocks, all of it penetrated by sunlight in patches as the lush trees create an otherwise full cover.

Among the growth sits the eponymous rock, sixty feet long and as wide and smooth as a paved roadway. The stream converges into rapids at the top and then fans out, like a slick coating of wax over the rock, until it spills into a deep, swirling green pool below. The National Forest Service has installed a set of iron railings to delineate a queue and prevent premature tumbles, as well as two separate observation decks from which people can hoot, holler or wince at the sliders. On the day we visited, a long line had formed at the railings while an audience watched from above.

Julie bounced up and down as we inched forward in the line up the rock face. She took her first descent without hesitation. She stayed in my lap as we hooted and hollered down the natural slide.

We plunged then from humid air into frigid waters. The water might have poured from a glacier. Its chill shocked us right out of our skin. As we paddled out of the pool, I asked Julie if she was okay. She regained her breath and looked back at the rock, realizing the scary and impressive thing she'd just done.

"Yes," she nodded slowly and then took to dancing on a nearby rock in her plastic swim shoes "Yes! Yes! Can we go again?"

So we got back in the line. As we approached the top, I settled into the rushing water once more, motioning for Julie to join me. But she froze. I took her hand and positioned her in front of me. She looked at the descent she'd just taken, as the water again tore past us down the massive rock. I felt her hands tensely gripping my knee. We were gradually slipping forward from our launchpad when she started squeaking "no, no, NO!"

It may have been the memory of the chilly dip awaiting us, but something had suddenly become frightening. She'd begun to overthink the sliding rock, which may be first on the list of don'ts when it comes to natural swim parks of this kind. It's sometimes best not to know what you're getting into. Ignorance can bestow courage. So maybe this was wisdom on her part.

- - -

I reviewed my itinerary so far. Cecile and I revisited the spontaneity vs. planning argument. I talked with several people about our trip, all of them advising against the interstate 10 Gulf Coast and Texas route. Given the time we needed to be in Arizona where we'd meet my family, we'd have to barrel through all of Texas in two days, which seemed a lot to ask of the girls and not fair to Texas either. I relented and changed the plans. We'd take the major artery I-40 through Arkansas and Oklahoma instead.

"Do you think you can handle this part of the trip not written down?" Cecile asked, a question I answered by placing my thoughts elsewhere.

We had to leave the Brevard campus before Yo-Yo Ma showed up. But I did get to sit in the amphitheater for one last rehearsal of Nina's orchestra. While Cecile was off with Julie, Louise and I took in a mini-concert, with Nina in the viola section and one of the hard-partiers from the previous night playing the violin, and with impressive gusto. Louise slept in her stroller, undisturbed by the sounds coming from the stage. The orchestra practiced a Dvořák piece for the upcoming weekend's performance. The conductor stopped and restarted the players often, which had the effect each time of underscoring the fullness of the sound being produced. An ocean of rising strings and clarion horns flowed from the stage, but when the conductor dropped his baton, it all came to an immediate halt. He gave instructions in a voice that was tiny and distant. Then he lifted his hands once more and the musicians swelled the ocean back up, carrying it across several measures before everything fell away again into the one small voice speaking.

The rehearsal revealed the intricate parts at work, making the unified noise created all the more astonishing. That my little sister, whom I remember at the same age of my own daughters in her own twirling pink dress and pigtails, happened to be one of the many pieces of this whole came as a more personal shock. Yo-Yo Ma couldn't have delivered this kind of spectacle.

We said goodbye to her that afternoon, leaving her surrounded by the music. We went west of Brevard on U.S. Highway 64, through the arm of North Carolina that reaches into Tennessee and Georgia. We never found ourselves on the Blue Ridge Highway during our trip, one of the first of dozens of places I pledged to come back to someday. However, U.S. Highway 64 provided the sights of the misty peaks, roaring waterfalls and deep green forests that add to this gorgeous part of the South and this road known as the Mountain Waters Scenic Byway.

Like the symphony interrupted by the conductor, rain poured off and on for the afternoon. The region was a wet jungle. Even when the sun poked through the storm clouds, mist enveloped the two-lane road and water dripped from the overhanging leaves and branches. We passed waterfalls spilling over black rocks.

Water seemed to be coming from everywhere. It was a beautiful way to start heading west, into these kinds of showers with the music of Dvorák still slipping in and out of my head. I could hardly stay neurotically focused on the road switchbacks and slick blind curves.

SAVE FOR FIREFLIES

We stopped at the Jackrabbit Mountain campground on Lake Chatuge, a lake spanning two states and featuring a thousand small inlets and peninsulas along its red clay shores. I'd read that, due to the higher elevation, Jackrabbit Mountain was cooler than the rest of the region. Since the heat felt sufficient for the baking of cake inside the glove compartment of the camper, I confirmed that we'd continue along the mountain route, rather than the bayou through the South.

We pulled into a site, sweaty and parched, ending the day's drive with a swim.

"Good thing America has lakes," Julie commented, her grinning face and orange swimmies bobbing on the surface.

After dark, I got out our new bug lantern. I told Julie and Louise that their job, before going to bed, would be to fill it with as many fireflies as they could.

"Yes! Yes! Yes!" they both hopped up and down, as I handed Julie the lantern and Louise the small plastic net that with went with it.

"Wait, Papa, I have a very good question," Julie stopped abruptly. "What's a firefly?"

They both looked up at me. Julie waited for an answer and Louise waited for Julie to be filled in and then provide the cue for them to both begin carrying on again. I had forgotten the firefly was a foreign creature to them. While species of fireflies existed in western Europe, they were less common in France and happened to be something they'd never been introduced to.

"Look." I pointed toward the shadows of the trees. "Do you see those tiny, blinking lights? They are called fireflies. They are bugs that know how to light up all by themselves!" Their eyes went wide at this wizardy of the woods.

Our campground was, by then, teeming with the silent bioluminescence of the firefly. They were everywhere, like the place had been showered with pixie dust. Julie and Louise rushed toward the insects as though they were the first two people on earth to discover them. Being the lethargic insects that fireflies are, the girls caught them by the handful, dropping them into the lantern, until the collective glow from behind the screen cast a yellow-green light around the lantern's base where it sat in the grass.

The girls spent the last of their daytime energy on the fireflies, with some leftover for bed-fidgeting, and eventually nodded off. Cecile and I cleaned off the picnic table and she followed the girl's lead. I sat down by myself in our camping chair to write.

I switched on my reading light that clipped to the camping chair. The tiny bulb piqued the interest of another breed of insect, the mosquito. So I switched it off and turned my attention to the campfire one site over.

A high school group had gathered for the night. School was out for summer and, apparently, forever. After an hour of giggling and guffawing, a fight broke out among two of the girls, over Garret, who evidently had been manipulated into falling for the one and not the other.

"Lindsay, you went behind my back!" an angry girl seethed, drawing out the "Y" and "I" sounds in a thick Georgia drawl.

The slighted person then threw someone's car keys, possibly Lindsay's, into the underbrush. Another consoling friend drove her off in one of the trucks. Following this, I could hear only stifled curses as the guys of the group stumbled over sticks and leaves, foraging in the brush for the keys.

This was a still younger set than the Brevard students and almost a full generation away from my college friends. I'd regressed through the Appalachians, old college friends in Virginia, current college kids in North Carolina and now high school unfurling along the Georgia border.

Was it possible I'd sought out this fountain-of-youth kind of journey? Was I fooling myself into thinking I was somehow a part of these people still becoming? Was there a connection to watching fireflies from my parents back porch when I was a teenager and the fireflies in my lantern now beside the group of teenagers from whom I hopelessly sat apart?

The trip thus far has been about revisiting. I'd been looking too closely at memories. Cecile had expressed this to me the day before by saying we needed to see more strangers. She was right. We needed more uncharted territory and new faces we had no past connection to. I would start, again, tomorrow.

For that night though, I still relished this scene. The American teenagers and the American fireflies. In ten years I might remember this blessed moment cushioned between my long-gone high school days and those of my own daughters still nestled in a hazy future. As I had with friends, with my sister's group and now witnessing the oblivious teens, I tried to appreciate this as the last goodnight to youth that might never be objective, or require my involvement again.

I switched off my reading lamp. The only light that remained was the dimming blinks of a few persistent fireflies inside our lantern. Those still roaming free had long ago turned off the spectacle.

Breakfast is an especially satisfying meal to eat in the outdoors, possibly because people rarely do. The cool morning air invited us to widen our eyes as the birds sang over our heads. Cecile drank from her portable French-press coffee mug with grounds she could toss into the dirt once she'd finished, while the girls drank their warm cocoa ("Cacao!" as they shouted for joy for all of nature to hear). I took swigs from my jug of multi-vitamin juice while serving out cereal for everyone. The girls were the quietest in the morning, we had by now noticed, a reversal of the rambunctious mornings in our apartment back home. They explored the edge of the woods coming back to us with collections of rocks, leaves and pinecones while we packed things up.

Next, they found the firefly lantern. Overnight, it had become less a lantern than a hand-held slaughterhouse. The fireflies all lay stone-cold at the base. Julie shed a few tears over them and we told her we'd find more that night.

Though, maybe it was best that none of us try catching and hanging onto fireflies. I would need particular psychic restraint to heed my own advice.

SAVE FOR FIREFLIES

Once the morning serenity had burned off along with the dawn mist and we'd done one last check of the site, the spot where we'd spent the night ceased to be ours. As we pulled out, we saw a couple of the high school kids, possibly just then turning in, strolling back to their tent. The boy held the girl's hand carefully as she led him back.

We returned to the familiar daytime rumble and roll of the camper. As usual, its motion put both girls to sleep, after only a few hours awake. Cecile read and then dozed herself. I put in my pre-made mix tapes and understood that we belonged on the road.

We passed a sign for Elkmont, a town and camping area in the Smokies. This location had an unusual distinction with regards to fireflies. Here, a phenomenon occurs that scientists can't explain. For several nights in mid-June, the fireflies of Elkmont light in unison. The account I read described hundreds of bugs blinking six times together before going dark again. Elkmont was one of only two places on the planet where such a natural, synchronized light show takes place, the other being in Malaysia. In either hemisphere, a more beautiful sight I couldn't imagine.

But, we wouldn't see it on this trip. We were just slightly late for the show. So I marked a place on the map to return to once again.

- - -

After five years in France, I'd forgotten how to talk. I was always a quiet type, but by my late twenties, I'd reached a point of gregariousness in social settings that was comfortable and breezy. To some, I was even quick-witted. However, just at the time my ability to make small talk like a real adult peaked, I was dropped into foreign territory where I was *demander*, rather than asked, where I would need to *regard* things rather than look at them, and where I didn't disturb others, but *dérange* them. Something would *blesse* instead of a wound and I checked a *séance* rather than a simple movie showtime. These cognates looked the same, but their meaning and pronunciation had gone screwy, pulling down with them my hopes for breezy communication.

Franco-American cultural differences were amusing and something I often used to my advantage, being the unusual person in the room and therefore, the source of everyone's curiosity and therefore exempt from embarrassment over social gaffes. The language, though, remained a slippery wall for me to scale. I'd never had much exposure to foreign languages growing up, like a lot of kids raised in central Pennsylvania. I'd taken Latin in high school. Also, with writing in my bones, I tended to think too much about the specifics and origins of words. As much as I loved them, I still didn't trust them, always looking for fluid meanings and peripheral connotations. While this worked well on screens and paper, I never had the knack for letting words flow from my head and smoothly out of my mouth. Somewhere in the process they always became garbled. For these reasons and also because I was no longer in my elastic-minded twenties, the linguistic carnage and horrifying confusion I'd left in the wake of my French learning curve was *profond* and *large*.

Cecile existed beside me as the polar opposite. She can enter another country where she doesn't know a word of the native tongue and, by the end of week, be gabbing with the locals in idioms and obscure street jargon without a hint of an accent. Her English is spoken like a true American, whose native region is only a little hard to place. Then when she goes to England, as she does often for business, she returns calling me *mate* and adding a lilt to the end of her questions. When I tell her to stop speaking to me like one of The Beatles, she wonders what I'm talking about.

In the home, among the four of us, we speak a loose Franglish. Julie asks me "Papa, can you passer the *sel*." Louise, at two, is comfortable with a babble all her own and Cecile and I do our best to speak only in our native languages when addressing the girls. Though, I often slip. I respond to Julie's question, "No, you have *trop* already."

As French has seeped into my conversating, it's also likely altered something fundamental about my perspective. One positive I've always appreciated lies in French greetings. Someone walks into a store and, systematically, no matter the circumstance or mood, whether a bakery, a nightclub, the police station or your grandmother's house, a person has a polite exchange that sets a solid foundation of courtesy. The greetings and responses are standard. I'd grown to count on it in France.

Not certain if I had a full grasp on any language, I found myself back in America. I entered a 7-Eleven and said "*hello*" to the guy behind the counter. He looked at me like my next step was armed robbery. "Hello?" he replied. "Can I help you?" My 'hello' caught him off guard. In turn, it caused me to second-guess. Was I not supposed to say anything? How did I walk into a convenient store during the first 28 years of my life? What should I say now as an adult?

I could use "Hey" or "Hi there" or "Hello, sir." I could also ask questions that were strictly meant to be rhetorical like "What's up?", "How you doing?" or "How are you?" that, if answered, would only confuse the other party. Concluding a conversation, I might offer "So long," "Take care" or "See you later," even if I had no intention of ever seeing that person again.

By late June, we'd made it to Alabama. We'd settled for a night in the Monte Santo campground in the town of Huntsville. At least, in the South no one gave you strange looks when you opened your mouth. In the communal bathrooms of the campground, as I shaved over the sink, a man waltzed in bellowing "Hey, boys, what's the good word?"

At first I thought he was talking to someone he knew, but another camper washing his hands beside me responded with the same geniality "Wish I knew. How 'bout yourself?"

"Yeah, I hear ya'," the easy-going fellow replied. We were all strangers, but therefore possible soulmates. The guy who'd just strolled in began whistling as he urinated, at one point reaching over for his toothpaste at the same time. The place had transformed into our home bathroom shared by a large extended family.

In the morning, we met some other campers on the campground loop.

"Hi! Yes hello, how are you doing, great day!" they smiled back at me, acknowledging every one of my greetings.

This group consisted of a family of two brothers with their elderly father, a retired naval officer, and one of the brother's toddler-age son. They'd come to attend the Blue Angels air show scheduled that day in nearby Huntsville. While our kids played together that morning we all talked about where we were from, the outrageous gas prices and how to keep the kids occupied in campgrounds.

"So what brings you to Alabama?" one of the brothers asked, wondering what a family like ours was doing in their neck of the woods. I explained where we'd come from and where we were going. After I finished, the older brother wondered "So wait, ya'll were born and raised in France then?" They had, understandably, mistaken me for French.

"No, no, she's French. I'm from up north," I said, which confused them. "You know, I'm just another yankee."

They laughed, the small self-effacing joke clarified the situation. They asked more about our trip, shaking their heads, as one brother added that his return drive to Tallahassee, Florida didn't seem so bad now. We exchanged more easy jokes and sincere wishes of further safe travels.

Cecile later said these guys were typical of Americans, treating us instantly as good friends. For me, I specified that it was typical of the South. Whichever group we assign this quality to, it was something we both appreciated. I was merely relieved to see my native language coming back to me.

"Take care!" I told them as we parted.

More Surprises in the South
* the well-designed and informative children's museum called EarlyWorks in downtown Huntsville, Alabama
* the extensive selection at the organic food store, Fresh Market, in Chattanooga, Tennessee
* the convenient store clerk who asked Cecile if she was Mexican when he heard her accent
* the morose look on everyone's face in chain restaurants like Chili's
* the friendly faces of those in Murphy, NC's Huddle House
* the vast size of the highway-side fireworks superstores
* the graphic images pro-life billboards juxtaposed, at the next mile marker, with equally graphic meth addiction ads
* the number of young people in Corinth, Mississippi's Wal-Mart with mohawks
* the ubiquity of pickup trucks that were sleeker and more modern, longer and higher off the ground than our camper
* that saying a name like Barack Hussein Obama to the vast majority of people we'd met would be more incomprehensible than speaking French to them
* that my printed itinerary didn't apply at all to the land I saw before my eyes
* that the long drives each day that still advanced us only a few inches farther west on the map
* that all of this was part of the same nation

SAVE FOR FIREFLIES

— — —

It occurred to us two days late that we were in the Central time zone. Being an hour behind everyone else hadn't affected us in the slightest. Time had become fluid.

The presence of a river had reminded us. We crossed the Mississippi, wide as an open plain and shimmering southward.

"Look everyone the mighty Mississippi!" I called out to my fellow passengers. They were not quite up to my level of enthusiasm on American icons.

But even my enjoyment of the country's epic waterway faded when we hit Memphis traffic. We inched over the bridge that carried us from the east into the west (and from Memphis into West Memphis, two distinct cities demarcated by the river). This was our first step into what I viewed as the beginning of the frontier and we were moving slower than a Conestoga wagon. I assumed the Mississippi was begging us to take it slow.

After the bridge, we connected with the major westbound artery we'd remain on for the next week, I-40. The traffic grew worse. We hit endless rows of eighteen-wheelers crawling at a mile an hour. An hour passed. We may have moved a car length. I turned on the radio seek feature, stopping at 94.1. Snap! The Rhythm of Memphis, so a DJ told us, playing club and dance music that got us energized again. The music gave us, at least, the illusion that we were cruising.

Cecile and I both spotted a Super 8 motel sign glowing a brighter yellow than the sunlight now losing wattage against the night sky. We said nothing. The absence of comment on the sign soon became a statement itself.

The Super 8 exit approached. Its sign also advertised a pool. Cecile and I nodded to one another. She turned to the girls, now banging their heads against the sides of their car seats.

"Is there anyone here who likes swimming pools?"

"Me!" came the unison response with little arms shooting into the air.

We pulled off the highway. The frontier had already conquered us.

The Super 8, for our tastes, was dirtier than a campground. When choosing between squatting over leaves and grass or the slightly cleaned toilet in our room, I'd go with the outdoors.

Julie and Louise had a broader, secondary bad reaction to the Super 8 that, after the relative luxury, manifested in revolt. That morning, we let them watch t.v. from the bed while we packed things up. They sat before the flicker with their standard unblinking zombie gazes.

When we were ready to go, Cecile stepped in front of the t.v. "Okay, time to turn it off." She looked at me. "Hey, put these bags in and start the car." Instead of doing the task, I reiterated what Cecile had said.

"Time to go, little peas!" I announced. I crept up to the television with my index finger extended and poked it into the power button. The screen blipped off. The whining rose from the bed. Louise tried to hide under the pillow.

"No!" Julie humpfed as she folded her arms like an affronted diva over her chest. She closed her eyes and turned her face toward the ceiling. I picked up Louise who grabbed the pillow and pulled it off with her. I had to pry it from her hands.

"C'mon, Julie. It's time. At the count of three, I want you off the bed. One, two..." Julie cracked her eyelids open to get a peek to see if I was serious. "Three," I deepened my voice, searching for more impressive levels of stern. After a pause, she burst suddenly out the door and into the camper.

Cecile looked at me annoyed. "I was handling it."

"Fine, but it doesn't matter who says it,right?"

"It's always you doing this."

"What are you talking about?" I replied annoyed, because I was sure I was helping.

"You're swooping in."

"Oh right," my voice took on more sarcasm and less of a tone of support than it had the night she'd been upset at the Virginia campground. I let her vent her worries, but my own stubbornness was peeking through. I became protective of my own marked territory with the girls and of the notion that I was in the right, having gotten the job done. I felt my own need to have my role as a father validated. But the right balance, particularly when it came to discipline, was easily tipped.

After Little Rock, the Ozarks stood for the great outdoors. We'd happened upon a campground in Fort Smith State Park in Arkansas, just east the Oklahoma border. Modern camping facilities had been established in this park only a year ago, with sparkling, clean bathrooms and showers and a large pool with a fountain designed for kids to splash in. All of it was 5-star when contrasted with the Super 8, yet with a secluded view through the trees onto the lake.

At dinner, I took to a timeless post: the fire. I hadn't yet perfected the campfire. I had a track record of four out of every five fires, whether in the campground fire pit or grill, ignited to sustainable roaring. This was a success ratio that would improve only slightly by the end of the trip. On this fourth time, however, I managed some billowing smoke and half-charred logs but little else. Here in the Ozarks, we had dry wood, a sack of twelve split pine logs purchased at a roadside convenient store and yesterday's newspaper. I'd placed gathered kindling in a teepee shape over balled up pages of the Arkansas Democrat-Gazette. After reading the news of Hillary Clinton teaming up with her recent rival on the campaign trail, I fed them to the flames. It wasn't a political statement, just all that we had.

The kindling got going slowly. I tried adding some of the smaller logs. They burned in patches. The fire never took on a life of its own. Fortunately, we didn't rely on the campfire to cook our evening meals. The marshmallows roasted after brief exposure to the burning pages of the Sports news of the local basketball team.

In the crepuscular light, I saw a family of six children heading down the path to the lake. The smallest one sat on the father's shoulders, hugging his stiff black baseball hat, while the oldest girl held the hand of one of the toddlers. The mother and four other children followed the father in an almost single file line. Aside from the younger boys bringing up the rear and swatting at plants with sticks, the whole group of eight barely made a sound. They'd also come from an RV that was only slightly larger than ours.

Two kids sometimes stretched my abilities as a parent to a breaking point. How did the dynamic of eight ever result in the kind of harmony I was witnessing? It must have been some strange Ozark mirage.

We'd see very few large families like this on the trip, people with one or two were the norm, and even fewer still who exhibited the peaceful, cohesive unit this family did. I watched them all heading down the path until they reached the lake and the boys began skipping stones. They were real, I concluded, and the simplest argument anyone could offer to the elasticity of the human heart.

By now routine, I stayed up after everyone else had gone to bed. Other campers had turned in to their RVs or switched off the lights inside their tents. I wrote in my journal beside my clip light. My watch read 9:19, finally adjusted to the correct time zone. It was a Saturday night. Most Saturday nights at this time, plans would just be gearing up or, at least, the television or computer would be keeping me awake for a few hours more. Here another rhythm took over. Within it, the irrelevant 9:19 was time to sleep.

I gingerly opened the side door to the camper to the sounds of three ladies breathing. Louise was currently occupying my spot on the lower bed, beside Cecile. She would start off there to prevent poking and giggling with Julie. Now that they were both deep into dreaming, I could transfer Louise up to the top bed.

I hoisted the slumbering two-year old bundle of Louise in my arms. I cradled her like an offering to the gods in my hands. I climbed the ladder into the cabover bed at the same time. None of this was graceful. Then, while balancing myself on the ladder, I had to ease Louise, feet first, onto the bed, cradling her still and sliding her in like I was putting a lumpy, oblong pillow back on a high closet shelf. A few months older and she'd have been too big to maneuver this way. On this trip, it was routinely the last activity I performed each day.

I pulled Louise's blanket up to her chin. I slid in between the sheets, missing for a moment the warmth of her fuzzy head and wrinkled pajamas that had just left my chest. I turned to give Cecile a kiss before falling asleep with them.

SAVE FOR FIREFLIES

WEST - - -

"So you're from New York then?"
"No. This is a rental. We live in France."
"France?!"
"But I'm originally from Pennsylvania."
"Oh..."
"My wife and I met in San Francisco actually."
"I see..."
"But now we all live in France."
"Uh huh..."
"The rental is from New York though, yes, like the plates say. It's where we started out our trip."

The fellow before me responded by silently adjusting his white cowboy hat, a way to express bafflement at the distance between the Texas-New Mexico border and New York City. Or else this was a reaction of general distaste for the three most pinko-commie liberal words in the English language: New York, San Francisco and France.

I shifted the focus. "What about yourself?"

It turned out he was from Amarillo which we could both make better sense of. His name was Kent. He was friendly and curious to a point, as long as the conversation didn't take his mind too far from the bucket of walleyes he'd caught during that day down at the lake.

Depending on the situation, I would pick one in the litany of places "we were from" and simply say that was our home. We were New Yorkers, San Franciscans, Parisians, Pennsylvanians, Dijonnais or refugees from the lost city of Atlantis. I had the repeated urge to pretend we were a transient family at home wherever we spread our plastic tablecloth. Among the widening expanses, the best pose to adopt as we moseyed our way through was that of rootless nomads.

Because we were now on the range. The mathematically flat horizon and the universe-sized sky. Working oil derricks and buffalo sightings. Indian gaming casinos and Indian trading posts hawking dreamcatchers and your name or favorite virtue engraved on a rock. I caved and bought the girls some Native American jewelry, though Julie was by now clinging most proudly to the black and red striped grasshopper she'd trapped in the bug lantern during our picnic lunch at a dusty Oklahoma park, a place that was notable for its breathtaking presence of a few trees. This sparse part of the country, with the pumps working away at the landscape, sold us the cheapest gas of our trip but still the most expensive I'd ever paid on U.S. soil.

I counted the West as beginning for us in the Red Rock Canyon area. This Oklahoma state park of bright red sandstone had rock walls rising from the prairie grass, like pieces of Utah's Arches National Park on a witness relocation program in the Great Plains. The canyon had served as a winter-dwelling for the tribes of the area in 1800s and then a resting point for pioneers and homesteaders setting out for California. It provided a cozy resting place for us, and only us on that night, as we saw few other campers aside from a group of climbers visiting to ply their hobby on the rock faces.

After conquering the Sooner state and the Texas panhandle, Kent from Amarillo greeted us at Ute Lake in the middle of high, dry northeast New Mexico. Kent would be our neighbor for the night. Once we'd exchanged our pleasantries and he'd checked his walleyes, he returned inside, leaving the afternoon sun for his customized cocoon of air-conditioning and daytime programming.

We, by contrast, went to the lake to swim beside the fish, neither to catch nor release them. Ute Lake, the name on the campground post, was nothing really, only a huge wet hole in the driest place I'd set foot on in years. But as we skipped toward it, we knew we'd found an oasis.

Ute Lake is thirteen miles long, one of the largest lakes in the state of New Mexico (not the most difficult superlative to achieve). From the dock and rocky sliver of beach at the base of the North area campground, all you see is one arm of it. It's hard to get a sense of its size. From our vantage point, it might have been a slowing, silty river.

The relief from the blowing heat made it paradise enough and I couldn't think of anywhere I'd rather be, at the moment, as we all splashed into these waters. I floated out further while Cecile and the girls fished around for rocks and submerged treasure just below the surface.

We were always aiming for water. This whole trip had been a daily quest to get into liquid. The plunge at the end of the day signaled home and safety for the night. For the girls, they spent a large part of their movement across the country asking when we'd be getting to the pool or the lake or the river or the ocean. We would dive into each one of them on the trip, under all kinds of circumstances. The pool at the Super 8, for instance, was as unremarkable as the rest of the hotel, but Julie and Louise squealed just as they had in a mountain lake or in a misty Blue Ridge waterfall. They heard a Poseidon call.

We stepped out of Ute Lake and walked back up the hill with the day's dust rinsed from our hair, the scorching heat momentarily defeated. The sun dropped to the other end of the plain and the wind picked up, galloping across the open stretch of earth born as a bluster somewhere in Kansas and swelled to a gale until it was bending skinny trees and knocking off hats in New Mexico. We ate dinner on the campsite table with rocks holding down our tablecloth. The cold air took over quickly at dusk which made the beds inviting for Julie and Louise. After a story with the two of them cuddled up on either side of me, I stepped out of the camper into the fallen darkness. The sky revealed stars even at the far horizon line.

The Milky Way lay across the night like the only cloud that wasn't moving.

"What are you thinking about?" Cecile turned to ask me the next morning.

We were going southwest on the arrow-straight Rte. 54 that cut a diagonal through New Mexico, heading across grandiose scenery of sagebrush with faded mesas and distant blue storm clouds gathering beyond them. My thoughts drifted to the other side of the canyon.

Cecile asked me the same question back at home, while I stared off into space with a soapy dinner plate in my hand or froze on a thought while folding socks. On the open highways, however, the space-cadet behavior not only suited the activity, but was encouraged as a way to pass the time on long hauls. The journey had given my reveries a purpose. I did need, however, the occasional nudge to pass a vehicle on the left.

But I never answered her question. I didn't have to.

"You're happy on the road aren't you?"

I smiled and nodded at her.

Cecile turned to the girls asked their opinions of the travels thus far. "*Et vous, les filles? Vous êtes contente sur la route?*"

"*Oui!*" they shouted back in unison, as we turned left in the center of the dusty town of Vaughan on 54 following signs to Alamogordo. If Vaughan was the worn but friendly outpost in the brush, Alamogordo was the sprawling modern metropolis. We drove in anticipation of one thing: White Sands.

At only nine a.m. the next morning, the horizon shimmered. I drove toward wobbly mirages. But the first thing I saw emerging from them was not the white dunes we'd come for, but the notification that we were entering the White Sands Missile Range.

In the heat, I assumed I'd read that wrong. Another sign confirmed it though. I double-checked the map to make sure we hadn't taken a drastically wrong turn. But this was correct. The dunes of White Sands, the 20 square mile area that makes up the preserved park, were abutted on the north and south by this military missile testing range.

The Trinity atomic bomb, one of the first detonations of a nuclear weapon, exploded here. The test went on to be employed as the real thing in the form of the 'Fat Man' bomb dropped over Nagasaki, Japan in 1944. This corner of New Mexico remains a nuclear testing ground. The road is still frequently blocked for safety reasons. It makes for a mixed introduction to a nationally designated treasure.

But, as if by deliberate contrast, we came upon the smaller section of white that had drawn us to this place. Bombs and radioactive fallout were meant to be forgotten. After passing the small visitor center and the ranger's booth at the entrance, I let the Cruiser Royale coast.

Entering the White Sands dunes was like gaining admission to the moon. The blank hills were snowdrifts that had spurned their physical compliance with the scorching sun and remained unmelted. The road cut through them, blown with powdery sand that covered the asphalt, obscuring the road's shoulder. This mattered very little though since, at all turns, there was nothing to crash into but soft white. We were now driving in a natural, oversized sandbox.

We parked along a turnoff inside the park, just beyond a boardwalk that had been set up to explore the dunes. We all took our shoes off and traipsed in. The texture of the sand was softer than any beach and much cooler. The girls, usually sensitive to heat, ran headlong across the expanse in bare feet. After a lifetime of scalding the bottoms of my feet on sunny beaches, I balked, thinking maybe we just couldn't feel the burn yet. But the White Sands dunes consist of white gypsum crystals which don't absorb heat. No scalding to speak of, no matter how hot the sun. It felt like walking on a warm carpet.

The girls went tearing up the mounds of sand and tumbling down the other side. We could let them roam pell-mell as far as they wanted. For at least a mile radius nothing blocked our view of them if we stood on the crest of one of the dunes. They both waved back at us to check they weren't doing something wrong. In the distance, on the left and right, I saw the tiny specks of other people exploring the place, a man taking pictures, a couple sitting, holding hands and another chasing through the hills and valleys like our kids. Still farther ahead, the faded San Andres Mountains marked the end of the monument and the beginning of the rest of the world from which we felt so set apart.

I also had two sleds. For a small fee, we'd rented plastic saucers and a soap bar-sized block of wax at the visitor's center. I selected a starting dune and called Julie over. She sat down in front of me and I grabbed the side handles as we took off. Showing none of the trepidation she showed at the sliding rock waters in North Carolina, here Julie immediately wanted to try it by herself. This plunge was easier all around, especially when compared to snow-sledding with its danger of ice patches and the melt that always seeps in through your coat and boots. Here we just had smooth, warm slopes before us that dusted our clothes and skin, transforming us into a family of friendly ghosts.

The only thing limiting our time at White Sands was the unyielding sun, which approaching late morning was beginning to sizzle. We retreated to a nearby picnic area. We found a ring of tables with C-shaped aluminum domes shielding the hungry and the sun-stroked. Fitted onto a slab of concrete, these picnic tables looked like parked moon rovers. We hopped aboard to eat salami and pickle sandwiches faster than we could make them and guzzled liquids. Louise finished and soon spotted a small white lizard, its skin bleached to blend with the environment, peering from around the corner of the aluminum structure. They both spent the rest of lunch insisting we catch and adopt him.

White Sands has been proposed as a world heritage site, which would bring into sharper conflict the fact that it is housed inside a missile testing range. The choice to me seems obvious, shut down the missile launch and make the whole region into a preserve. But I'm looking at the simpler picture. The missile testing area is chosen, of course, because of the low impact on the surroundings. There also might be something to my impression that the desolation and tragedy of the bomb site heightens the beauty it envelops.

Still, did anyone but my daughters, bother to ask the lizard his opinion?

More of the day would unwind into the wondrous and the absurd. On Hwy 10 out of Las Cruces, we were pulled over. Border patrol needed us to stop.

"Did we take a wrong turn into Mexico?" I asked aloud, decelerating.

"I don't think so," Cecile replied. She doublechecked the map.

An officer approached my window and, instead of waving us through, told us to get into the other queue.

I asked the next officer if we'd arrived at the border. He humorlessly responded no and explained that this was an interior border check. He asked us to open the side door where he stepped inside for a quick look around. Evidently any vehicle that looked like it could smuggle several bodies at once required closer inspection.

"Is everyone in this vehicle a U.S. citizen?"

"Well, no. Not my wife."

The officer's laser-beam gaze shot to Cecile.

"Can I see your passport please?" he continued.

When she handed over the brown French passport, he looked puzzled. His battle-ready stance dropped upon realizing she was European, which didn't count.

He asked for details of the girls and by the time I got into explaining they both had dual citizenship, he'd fully lost interest. We, however, were still on edge. My mind raced over possible violations starting with the time I stole a pack of gum at age six from a local supermarket to the unpaid overdue fee I'd left on my Blockbuster video card upon leaving for France to all the documents we'd ever filled out concerning customs, visas, citizenship and patriotic duty to, finally, the packet of Roman Candles that I'd purchased at a small roadside fireworks stand now stashed in the overhead cabinets. We, who had little to worry about, somehow ended up being the most jumpy. I couldn't imagine what I'd be feeling were we actually involved in some sort of border violation.

We proceeded through Estados Unidos de América cautiously.

Again, nature reassured us. We came upon another natural oddity: the City of Rocks. I'd read about the place and researched pictures on Google Earth and ReserveAmerica interactive maps. I had, then, staked a claim through an encrypted credit card reservation. I had printed out the confirmation page which read site number 8 at the City of Rocks State Park campground. In this way, I was almost exactly like all the pioneers, outlaws and homesteaders who'd crossed this land before me.

City of Rocks stood as a formation of rock columns and boulders shaped by a volcanic eruption almost 35 million years ago. Off the highway, I saw the "city" rising in the distance on a gradual slope. Boulders resembled stone giants huddled together on the hillside, some tall with broad shoulders, others squat and gashed with holes. Throughout the central clump of rocks, pathways and alleyways had formed. This has created secluded and enclosed spaces for tents and campers. At various spots, ground had been leveled to accommodate RVs.

The only permanent inhabitants for miles, aside from the jolly campground host with her belt pulled way up, were jackrabbits, hundreds of them in the camping area alone. I knew of a size differential between jackrabbits and the common cottontail, but didn't know the degree. Louise spotted rabbit ears peeking up over a spiky bush and walked toward the furry friend she'd figured she could cuddle with. But when the monstrous jackrabbit crept out from behind the shrub, sniffing the ground and not frightened away in the least, Louise stopped in her tracks at the muscled rodent larger than a housecat.

Meanwhile, wasps hovered around the top of our camper as storm clouds swirled in the distance. We ducked for cover inside. Blasts of wind whipped around the rocks as we all huddled in the camper's back bed to wait out the weather. The sun was soon entirely blotted out by charcoal gray clouds. Out of the back window, we could see a curtain of rain sweeping across the barren valley. The water dragged the rain clouds down to the earth. Drops pelted our roof, starting on an intermittent drumbeat and increasing to a heavy downpour. But it lasted for only five minutes. One last furious gust of wind walloped the camper. I heard a bang just outside our door.

"What was that?" Cecile gasped.

We both looked up and then to the stony ground. The plastic cover to our air conditioning unit had blown off and crashed to the ground. The faded words DuoTherm knocked against the campsite's fire ring.

"Oh...*mon dieu.*"

I stepped outside and grabbed the large dome of plastic before the tail-end of the storm carried it off. A large crack ran up one side. An entire corner was missing where it had snapped off from its fastening bolt.

"At least that didn't happen while we were driving." I told Cecile through the open window of the camper as she and the girls watched the man who wears the pants in the family cradling a piece of their summer home in his hands.

Then, I noticed the wasps. Yellow jackets were circling faster now around the top of the camper. They had doubled in number. They seemed to be orbiting the spot where the piece of our camper had just come dislodged. I stepped up onto the nearby the picnic bench to get a better view. Attached to the now uncovered aluminum coils was a papery, mud-gray wasp's nest. The buzzing insects wiggled in and out of the tiny combs built into their nearly-completed structure, an organic version of the near-operational Death Star from Star Wars. I had now uncovered my own miniature imperial fleet. And they were all enraged that their plans had been revealed.

  I flashbacked to the place I'd seen these things before. Back in Brevard, North Carolina, over two weeks ago, one of the cabins had a nest that had formed under the back porch overhang. I remember my sister saying that no one had worked up the courage to get rid of the nest. We'd parked the camper in a spot near this cabin on our last night in Brevard. These wasps must have been in the market for a satellite location. They'd chosen the big white mass that had shown up out of nowhere and started construction under the flimsy plastic cover. From there, they'd clung tightly while moving at 60 miles an hour through heat and lashing wind. I thought back through all the moments we had with our camper between North Carolina and here, now with the addition of stingy company I didn't know we had.

  Julie and Louise heard the talk about wasps and wanted to see, but Cecile kept them corralled inside with the windows tightly shut. The girls pressed their faces to the glass. I went looking for the longest stick I could find;

coming back with something that wasn't long at all but was the best the low brush of the area could offer. I paused.

Were these yellow jackets or a mutant breed of southern wasps? Was there a difference? Wasps, like yellow jackets and hornets, released a distress signal pheromone. When this signal was near the nest, the whole group launched into attack mode. Also, unlike honeybees, they were capable of multiple stings. I was now overthinking.

I batted away the hive like a piñata with awful prizes inside. It crashed to the ground at my feet. I darted in the opposite direction. Upon reaching a safe distance, I abruptly downshifted into a nonchalant stroll so as not to launch the distress signal of my fellow campers. I whistled something tuneless like I was in a sudden hurry to check out this part of the campground. The wind rolled the fragile nest across the rocks and scattered these Blue Ridge mountain insects across the unforgiving, arid sprawl of their new frontier. From inside the camper, the ladies I was trying to protect stared back at me, slightly perplexed. I told them the wasps were gone, much to Julie's disappointment.

Nightfall dropped the temperature dozens of degrees. I sighed like it was the first steady breath I'd taken since morning, making it hard to view the day as nothing but the fullest I'd had in recent memory and the network of stars in the sky as nothing but a light-year's distance closer than I'd ever felt them to be.

- - -

I repaired our broken cover with duct tape and two bungee cords, like only a true professional would. I scraped off the traces of the nest from the air conditioner and inspected all parts of our vehicle for further evidence of winged infestations. I placed an incensed phone call to the rental agency rep about the flimsy cover. They responded with weak apologies.

So we shoved off from the City of Rocks campground before the sun reached its 10 A.M. scorch. I felt as though something had been conquered, something had been survived and nature hadn't bested us yet.

The date was July 4. We crossed more eternal desert spaces until we reached the larger town of Silver City, once a gunslinger and stagecoach waypoint but now a mid-sized community with holiday traffic, Wal-Mart and fast food chains along main street. We parked in the lot of a Sonic Burger and walked toward the sound of a drumline and horns.

Independence Day had begun.

The marching band had a handful of mesmerizing drummers and the sombrero-donned Mexican riders trotted on horses who'd been trained to move sideways. The high school baseball teams nodded their heads to hip-hop in large, menacing packs from atop their undecorated floats, while the local Army Reserve brandishing weapons in full fatigues were followed, shortly after, by the local peace activists, a much smaller group including an amputee vet carrying a sign that said "Healthcare not Warfare."

Julie and Louise, for their part, were fully sold on the entire show at first sight of the baton twirlers in the sparkling leotards doing flips and synchronized tosses. They mimicked the moves from the sidelines until the twirlette coach bringing up the rear showered the crowd with lollipops. Lined on both sides to the right and left of the street, people sat on the curb or in lawn chairs, eating snow cones and waving small star and stripes on little sticks. Cecile, like me, was glad to have found a place to see a parade for the occasion, but mostly happy for the girls. She was never the type to indulge in any country's nationalistic pride.

I sat down to enjoy our own snow cones. At the moment though, it was irrelevant to me that we were celebrating a national holiday. I couldn't get patriotic about the day. I had trouble with the God Bless America fever everyone else had caught. Surrounded by these people giddy about America's 232nd birthday, I felt oddly ostracized from the party. I felt like a foreigner.

I was intruding on the anniversary of the founding of a club whose membership I hadn't ever chosen, though I'd defended it endlessly and couldn't wait to return to it when I was outside its borders. Here, back in the fold again, I watched the floats pass by feeling lucky to know this was only the 4th consecutive day in the 7th month of the year everywhere else in the world.

Something amiss in the American brand of patriotism. Having by this point crossed a healthy portion of the nation, I couldn't shake the thought now that the standard form of over-exuberance missed the entire point of what is great about the United States. We are the only country I know of where citizens routinely chant in unison their three-letter national abbreviation. And something about repeating that America is number one loses all its meaning (regardless of its accuracy in any respect) when the statement is uttered by people who've never spent any amount of time learning about the other places America is that much greater than. I tried to imagine a group of French people in the streets waving their tricolor flag and declaring *"Nous sommes numero un!"* and how it would give me the shivers. I won't even get into the kind of images conjured if I encountered a similar group of Germans.

I'd seen more rabid patriotism in spectacles back in Pennsylvania or blasted over television airwaves from political rallies. In Silver City, a sizable portion of the parade-goers were not speaking English. At only 40 miles from the Mexican border, this was no surprise. This fact alone restored meaning to the occasion, making America a place that was strived for, fought for and endlessly dreamed of. They didn't take their inclusion in the day as a given, but rather a blessing.

Nonetheless, what makes any country number one is never what we spend time touting in public assembly. After the parade, we settled down at the Manzano RV campground, on the outskirts of town. Bob and Maria Manzano welcomed us like old friends, like we belonged even though, we'd learn, we were the only campers present under the age of 60. They invited us to the evening potluck dinner, where the campground sat down together as a family.

On the Manzano family porch, we met Mary from Jackson, Mississippi who explained how she could never live in a bricks-and-mortar house again. She and her husband had tried the year before, but only lasted a month before needing to sell the place and get back on the road again living out of motorhome.

We met Arthur, a tall, blocky man with huge square glasses, and his wife, who never said a word. They were from Massachusetts and didn't recommend Monument Valley. "You can try, be my guest, but those backroads are no place for an RV, I can tell you that," he threw up his arms too early for us to explain we'd stay on the main roads.

And we met Frank with slicked back hair, a full-throated laugh and a cigarette forever in his mouth. The woman he sat close to introduced herself as Linda. Frank turned out to be from my hometown of York. He hadn't lived there in years and now split his time between here and Pensacola, Florida. We went over familiar names and places, having trouble believing that we'd both somehow crossed paths all the way out here. Once we'd exhausted the exchange of hometown landmarks and came up empty on any mutual acquaintances, we were unsure of where the conversation should go. Something more should be made of this coincidence. We both shook our heads.

"Wait'll I tell my family I met someone out here from York!" I said.

"Yeah, that is something!" he replied. There the conversation stopped.

Common ground or not, the older company made us feel taken care of. After my tour through the various incarnations of youth in the east, the enveloping presence of an older generation made for a cozy respite.

Far from the fanfare of the 4th, we retired to our campsite early, in keeping with the habits of our early-to-bed fellow campers. Cecile and I sat outside then like an old married couple, our four years of marriage at once transformed into forty, reading magazines and listening to the sounds of fireworks popping in the night sky launched from a party elsewhere, where all the supposed action was.

- - -

Things Found In My Cargo Shorts Pockets After Three Weeks
* wallet and car keys
* three rainbow barrettes
* half a roll of Butter Rum LifeSavers, top piece covered in lint
* Swiss army knife
* a small stone from the ground in the City of Rocks that had been struck by our fallen roof
* a lighter with an Arkansas Razorback mascot on it
* a tissue used to wipe Louise's nose balled up inside the empty plastic Kleenex packet
* a Chili's lunch coupon for half off on kids' meals
* 1 dollar and 38 cents in dimes, nickels and pennies
* an energy bar crumbled to dust inside its unopened packet
* ketchup and mustard packets swiped from a gas station condiment stand

I moved much of the inventory from my pockets to the space under the driver's seat. In a Tupperware box, I'd stashed more granola bars and a bag of hard candies that I'd eaten too many of already. But the principal use of the box was to hold the cassettes. After several weeks, I no longer found it strange to be rewinding and fastforwarding on a tape again. The outdated stereo of the vehicle felt just right for the trip.

I pressed play on an old song, "I Love the Mountains," that I once listened to as a kid in summer camp. We would sing the tune in rounds in front of campfires, with the refrain "I love the mountains, I love the rolling hills, I love the flowers, I love the daffodils, I love the fireside when all the lights are low…" The camp counselors with their acoustic guitars would get more into this than the wee campers, who waited impatiently through the belted-out song for the s'mores to be broken out.

I hadn't heard the song since. But I'd discovered it on a kid's music compilation CD of Julie's shortly before our trip. Upon hearing the tune again, the memory of the campfire circle came back clearer than a digital photo. Music funneled all my senses into this long dormant memory. This time, I sang along, as the peppy camp counselor. This transformation was partially a joke on my part. Partially not. In turn, the girls became the yawning kid I once was.

But, once I shut up about it, everyone enjoyed the music. Louise repeated words "Fahwers, Papa!" Julie picked up the melody with effort. Soon, Cecile requested her own selection from another kid's tape, one of her and the girls' favorite "Sur le Pont d'Avignon" a beloved French standard. Once we changed selections, Cecile transmogrified into a sprightly French choral instructor, ready with hand motions and exaggerated voices for the various song characters.

We swayed to the anthem of the south of France, as we crossed the continental divide. We followed the flow, like all the rivers now, due west.

Deep into the land where states stretched out and enlarged to three-times their recommended size, I wanted to take a meandering road from Silver City into Arizona and perhaps make it all the way to Monument Valley before sundown. I knew, as we climbed toward Arizona, that this was ambitious.

We left the desert behind for the alpine mountains (cue camp song) of the Apache-Sitgreaves National Forest that straddled the Arizona and New Mexico border. The trees were spaced further apart, unlike the dense, overgrown forests of the east, and looked hardy enough to beat the daylights out of the delicate maple or birch of my old backyard. We passed several fenced-in areas with cows grazing among the pines, offering the beautiful juxtaposition of a ranch in the woods. We stopped for a picnic by a mountain lake, after which we descended into the long stretches of vast dry grasslands of Arizona.

Following the daily routine, the girls then drifted off to sleep. It was also typical that Cecile reclined in her passenger seat and asked if I was okay driving while she napped "for just five minutes."

My mind lay far from slumber on these afternoons. It was a time of the day I looked forward to. I waved to a pair of cyclists passing on our left. I turned up just slightly the non-kids music I'd chosen.

From my driver's seat, this was meditation. This was a highway and country that might be moving under our wheels, while we remained in place. These moments at this particular helm revitalized me like no nap could.

By late afternoon, we'd connected back up to the truck corridor that is Interstate 40. The girls woke up and Cecile with them. She handed out snacks- a banana, a yogurt drink and some fish crackers. I continued with the mix of jangly indie rock which was always hit-or-miss as family entertainment. I switched to happy techno and then campfire songs and finally the failsafe Disney princess soundtracks, but the moment for music merging with our travels had passed for the day. Whimpers, whines and bursts of yelping threatened to overtake all else.

"How far to Monument Valley?" Cecile asked, a hint of her own restlessness creeping into the question.

"We can make it."

"Ok good," she replied, restlessness no longer disguised, "but how far?"

"We can be there in three hours."

"Three hours!?"

"Ok, two then. There's no good place to stop along this highway."

"It's getting worse in the back," Cecile reported over the rising discontent coming from behind us. I heard Louise knocking her head against the side headrests of her car seat.

Julie shouted out a request for another snack which was stiffly denied as Cecile scratched her head over the map and a Southwest campground guide. The girls began the launch sequence leading to full-tilt dual tantrums. I heard the thwack of coloring books and crayons being chucked to the floor. Julie whined at higher pitches. Louise cranked up to a siren-like wail. For them, at this very moment in time, they were clearly trapped in their seats for the rest of their lives. The apocalypse was upon us.

The noise rose to something that could crack fissures in the windshield. It pounded against the inside of my skull. It derailed concentration, it mocked patience and goodwill. I'd read that recordings of children crying were, at the time, being played on a continuous loop for prisoners at Guantanamo Bay, as a particularly devious and untraceable form of mental torture. It was a shame that I could understand how sadistically clever a device this was. It made me want to scowl like the then Vice President.

These girls were able to be the most beautiful creatures ever to set foot on earthly soil, while also having the ability to emit cries and screams that were among the most demonic. It was a sound that only we could fully appreciate. It was a sound developed solely for us, to locate and stab at our most sensitive nerve. And this was how nature intended it.

Cecile tried more diversions to no avail. Then, we turned to disciplinary action. Cecile raised her voice and warned of further punishment if this kept up. I seconded with a lecturing tone, further highlighting our general ineffectiveness. Cecile slumped back into the passenger seat. She and I tried to communicate over the noise.

"YOU WANT ME TO PULL OVER!" I yelled.

"NO, JUST IGNORE THEM!" Cecile shouted back.

"I DON'T THINK WE'LL MAKE IT TO MONUMENT VALLEY!"

"WE CAN'T GIVE IN TO THIS KIND OF BEHAVIOR!"

"THEY NEED TO LEARN!"

"YES! BESIDES, THEY NEED TO LEARN"

"SOON, I'M GOING TO START CRYING TOO!"

"HOW DO WE GIVE A TIMEOUT AT A CAMPGROUND?"

"OK!"

"ANYWAY IT'S NOT REALLY THEIR FAULT!"

"MAYBE SOME DVORAK CONCERTO MUSIC WOULD DO THE TRICK!"

"WE'VE BEEN ON THE ROAD FOR ALMOST SIX HOURS!"

"NOW YOU'RE EXAGGERATING!"

"JULIE'S KICKING MY SEAT!"

Enter the KOA. Kampgrounds of America is the largest chain of campground facilities in the country. As the girls wore themselves out with the hysterics and as Cecile and I successfully attained dementia, we saw the yellow sign with the red and black teepee for the Holbrook KOA Kampground near the Petrified Forest. We exited the highway. We assured the girls, and ourselves, that this would be over soon.

It would be our first experience with the KOA. The K was for konvenient or kommerical or kompromise. A friendly KOA staffer, decked out in a walrus-like mustache and a mustard yellow Polo shirt, greeted us at the camp entrance. He gave us a quick rundown of the fun things to do, tours of the fossilized remains of the Petrified Forest or the historic landmarks of Route 66 or a "cowboy cookout" for breakfast the next morning. But we passed on the organized fun. We just needed a quiet place to let the steam out of the camper.

I drove to a parking spot with the number 34 on it. I wondered if maybe we'd wait here until being shown to our site. As it turned out, the space, sandwiched between two 30 ft. mobile homes with a view onto the highway in front of us and a Burger King behind, was, in fact, our site.

But the girls' mood had instantly changed. Cheeks still wet with tears, they'd both spotted the playground where some kids batted around a tetherball and others teetered on seesaws. Then they saw the pool. Julie hopped up and down saying "Pool! Pool!" until Louise understood and hopped along with her. The apocalypse was over. Our world could begin anew.

We swam and frolicked the evening away in a modest "campground" with K. No one recalled that only hours before we'd all witnessed our collective ruin.

The KOA had well anticipated our road weariness, like thousands of traveling families before us. The next morning, we learned that the main advantage of this market-monopolized chain of campgrounds beside convenience would be the people we met. The communal family atmosphere made up for the general non-beauty around us.

We met several families, a retired couple from Wyoming taking their grandson on a summer vacation and a family from Orange County with three teenagers grudgingly in tow. The morning sun rose over the outdoor "cowboy cookout" that consisted entirely of pancakes. We were all here.

Then I heard French spoken somewhere out of the clear blue sky.

"*Comme c'est beau,*" a woman's voice murmured behind me. I was the only cowboy who looked up from my plate of shortstacks.

She stood before a petrified tree trunk, an ancient, formless hunk of wood I wouldn't have thought to describe as "*beau.*" At its base, a tiny plaque proclaimed its age at a hundred million years, with the rings to prove it.

"*Merveilleux!*" the woman reaffirmed.

Her words, along with the idea that this Painted Desert fossil was beautiful, came from elsewhere. It reminded me that I was only a tourist myself.

We introduced ourselves and exchanged our stories of what we were doing here. I was just glad I hadn't forgotten every word of the French language after all the meandering around America.

<u>Things a Family of French Tourists Told Us about America</u>
* they were very excited to visit the reservation today
* they couldn't wait to get to Santa Fe (reason not given)
* all the Americans they'd met had been warm and generous

* the highway patrolmen who'd stopped them for speeding was a little frightening
* the fresh air of the country made them feel young
* they hadn't found a place that served real coffee yet, but hadn't given up hope
* they'd heard of Pennsylvania and had always wanted to get there someday
* their teenage daughter wanted to move to Las Vegas after she finished school
* you could never find a place for breakfast like this in France
* you could never find gas this cheap
* that there must be some tourist bureaus where people spoke French, *non*?

    I explained I was born and raised in the U.S., which they'd figured. But now I was a visitor, a temporary repatriate or some kind of darling clementine. I explained I'd been away long enough that I worried the U.S.A. had transmogrified into a place nearly foreign to me.

    Pouring myself more watery coffee, I said that we'd met warm and generous folks too, but also more pessimists than I'd remembered. It seemed Americans were worried about the future of their country. I was worried about this. We were headed in the wrong direction.

    She smiled saying I sounded negative. France was supposed to be the place for pessimism. No one wants to see Americans feeling discouraged.

"Besides," the mother of the family added, "where else but in America can you eat pancakes outside, and with berries that are blue?"

We wished each other happy trails and *bonne continuation* and went our separate ways. I stood up with a toothpick in my mouth and realized I'd just received a chin-up American dream pep talk from a French woman. Surely, she was doing this just for my benefit. She must have known this was what I wanted to hear.

"Did I sound negative?" I asked my wife.

"*Un peu,*" she replied, sending the kids skipping toward the nearby plaground, "but this is what I've been trying to tell you this whole time."

Over by the sandbox and monkey bars, we met a family from Phoenix. They were on a trip to Colorado with their kids, close in age to ours.

Our conversation extended beyond parenting tales when the father told me he was a paramedic who ran helicopter patrols along the border just south of Tucson. He told us the area was the most heavily crossed segment of the shared U.S.-Mexico border. He listed the dangers of border crossing- dehydration, sunstroke, snake and scorpion bites as well as the risks of skirmishes between rival smugglers and drug traffickers and, on occasion, vigilante border patrol groups. He told a story from earlier that summer of a pregnant woman who went into labor while trying to cross the river. He nearly choked himself up as he recalled the incident for me. We both looked to our own kids and our wives, sharing lighter stories about potty training.

While hearing these tales, my mind raced.

My Sequence of Thoughts About Immigration in America
* the intimidating stare of the New Mexico border patrol officer
* a photo I'd seen recently of a Mexican woman stopped by customs who'd been squeezed into the hollowed out area of a car's glove compartment.
* the Spanish-speaking families at the 4th of July parade
* our own complaints when we had to fill out visa paperwork or wait in long lines at the U.S. embassy or customs for Cecile
* the following question Cecile was asked to answer 'yes' or 'no' to at airport customs: Have you ever been or are you now involved in espionage or sabotage; or in terrorist activities; or genocide?
* my own ancestors' journey from Germany and England
* Europe's immigration problems that lacked the dream component with the grand visions of realizing one's potential
* how this made America's own immigration realities that much crueler in the end
* the fact that, according to 2000 census data, 1 out of every 5 people in the U.S. speaks a language other than English in the home
* how we would be one of those homes if or when we moved back
* that we had a relatively simple path back in
* that the whole country rested on the foundation of people aching and dying to get into the country

* that I'd known for five years what it was like to live as a foreigner in another country, but hearing the eyewitness accounts of this paramedic, I realized I didn't have the faintest idea what the yearning to find a better life elsewhere actually meant.
* how this French mother and Cecile both said Americans like me shouldn't get discouraged

The next day behind the wheel the country moved, itself in flux beneath our wheels. Abruptly, north of highway 40 toward Monument Valley, the commerce disappeared from the land.
We passed the occasional clump of rundown homes plunked down in barren soil and the infrequent poorly-maintained gas station. We had the feeling of being in a bleaker corner of Mexico. Only we weren't. We were in a particular region inhabited by the only non-immigrant peoples of the country. This was Native American land.
The Navajo territory of northeastern Arizona is the largest area of land under internal sovereign jurisdiction. From the road we were on heading north toward the Utah border, we saw very little of the Navajo communities. The town of Tuba City offered a slight uptick in apparent vibrancy. But this isolated nation was marked along the road by the hand-made signs for things like "Real Indian goods" or "Authentic Navajo artifacts" and sometimes a trailer or two off in the distance with a plastic swing set standing in the dirt. I saw a traditional log-shaped home called a hogan sitting on a hilltop and couldn't ascertain if it was in use by the Navajo or was simply a roadside attraction, or existed as

some combination of the two. A gleaming SUV with the words Navajo Nation Police decaled on its side drove by. Never mind that these officers were driving a Jeep Cherokee.

We stopped at one the gas stations, where a hungry-eyed dog shambled around the camper while a man in a jean jacket leaning against a wall stared vacantly back at us. Inside the grim and half-stocked supermart by the station, we bought four Freeze Pops on which I noticed the warning "Not for Individual Resale." The vendors here were doing what they could.

None of this exactly matched up with Pocahontas, the girls' beloved princess from the Disney film of the same name who fell in love with John Smith and halted all fighting between the white man and the Indian with a single swoosh of her flowing black hair. The animated Pocahontas was by now an unfortunate reference point to what we saw around us. Not that the legions of other travelers old enough to know better didn't fall into the same trap. It proved to be a problem throughout much of the West, trying to reconcile the real and complicated history with the cartoonish, image of a mystical and peaceful people in touch with the earth. The dilemma of presenting the tragic history while celebrating what we could wouldn't end here.

As if by a matter of course, we came to the cowboy portion of the story. Out of the red dust, the horizon pushed up huge isolated red buttes. We approached Monument Valley, the pillars of the classic Western, where all other spur-jangled horizons, untrammeled ranges and endless American skies commenced. The striated sandstone buttes shaped like giant mittens rose from city block-sized mounds of earth. In the distance, they met up with more extensive ridges. The monoliths gave the valley between them an even more pronounced emptiness, as though something should exist between them.

It's no wonder why the filmmaker John Ford was inspired to run a stagecoach through this valley and capture it on film. He shot his first film here in 1939 with John Wayne called by that very name, *Stagecoach*. He then returned to film nine more at the location, including *The Searchers, Fort Apache, My Darling Clementine* and *He Wore A Yellow Ribbon*. The iconic Monument Valley scenery continued to be cemented in the minds of modern audiences with *Back to the Future III, Forest Gump* and *Thelma and Louise* and, at least, a dozen car and running shoe commercials. It also was the backdrop chosen for French comic books like the gunslinging Lucky Luke, French travel agency ads for *Aventure en Amérique*, and the panorama at the faux-dry goods store in Frontierland at Disneyland Paris.

At the Goulding's Museum and Trading Post, we were treated to exhaustive displays of every other instance in which the valley has been put on celluloid, along with memorabilia from the sets and crews. The museum and all other shops and restaurants in the area were staffed entirely by the Navajo and any information about the cowboy legends created here was systematically offset by a display of the Navajo history at the same point in time.

We settled into the Goulding's campground (the family that introduced John Ford to the area and since seemed to have cornered the tourism market of the region). Based on the other visitors to the valley and all the campers we shared the evening with, no other group seemed to be more enthralled to witness the mythic American West come to life than the Europeans.

At the check-in booth, two teenage boys pointed out, in Swedish, the features of a geologic wall map of the Colorado Plateau. Along the short trail to a natural arch overlooking the valley, one German couple asked another to take their photo, *bitte*. Beside our campsite, an older man questioned in a Scottish accent if they might try the lodge. Somewhere nearby, I overheard more French, mixed possibly with the words coming from my wife's mouth. Cecile whispered to our daughters as they gazed out from the high vista we reached at sunset, *"Regardez bien."*

The shadows of passing clouds crawled over the valley floor of scrubby brush and red dirt. In the far distance, a faded purple butte stood like an unattainable citadel of stone. There was no denying the magic. Still, Cecile was seeing something deeper.

On one of my first days in France, Cecile and I walked the hill of Montmartre to the steps of the Sacré-Coeur church. I knew only a few words in French at the time and kids were still a figment for us. On that day, the city felt like an oil painting I'd been allowed to climb into. From the top of the hill over the network of star-patterned boulevards, I thought that the French had created a place that was beyond all my understanding of beauty. I remember Cecile being primarily happy to watch me watching it. She knew which part of this vision was only an illusion, while I bought into it fully.

Now it was her turn. She stood before the valley-wide possibilities of America and its manifested destiny, without irony, here to measure herself within it as a lonesome cowgirl.

The iconic skyline of Monument Valley had drawn the Europeans, after enduring lines at immigration, the guilty-until-proven innocent questions and the smirks and slack jaws at their accented English. But once inside, Monument Valley was there for the taking all over again. The Americans didn't belong here anymore than they did. This made it easier to marvel at the places where the country exposed its bones. For Americans, it took a little more concentration to remember that the land united all the way out to here was the wildest idea anyone ever had.

As Simone de Beauvoir observed in her travels, as she passed by train through northeastern Arizona, "These blind plateaus gently baked by sun exist, with a splendid stubbornness, for themselves." Despite the convergence of states, a tribal nation and a constitutional republic, this place still existed for itself. It would forever keep wide-eyed intruders coming from miles. It would forever keep others coming back.

On this first stop in the Grand Circle of the Southwest, we could be, like everyone else, both dumfounded foreigners and swaggering natives. We could belong.

The spaciousness of Goulding's campground, where we'd spend the night, didn't exactly match its surroundings. The sites were like the KOA's. RVs parked together with scarcely enough room to fully open the driver's side door.

Most of the other units present were the boxy Cruise America 28 foot rentals, twice the size of our camper, sporting blown-up photographs along their sides of the very place the vehicle was currently touring. We had pulled in without a reservation that mid-afternoon and, out of sheer luck, had been assigned the site at the far corner. To the left of our camper, one massive Cruise America blocked our view of all other RVs, while to the right we had our picnic table beside a low fence that provided the unimpeded views out toward the valley.

    For dinner that night, we took ingredients we had in the camper fridge that would soon go bad and combined them in a large bowl. We improvised a salad, even for the girls who were difficult sells when it came to fresh vegetables. We decided to name it and remember the recipe. I pretended it was exactly what a cowboy would eat out on the range. We pretended some more, as the light went out over the valley, that our trip had just then begun.

<u>Ingredients to Monument Valley salad</u>
* 2 or 3 diced avocados
* 1 whole cucumber peeled and diced
* 1/2 cup of black olives
* corn cut from 1 cob
* 1 can of chick peas
* 1 cup of chopped cilantro
* tossed with balsamic vinegar and olive oil

We woke the next day to an insistent sun.

"You mean, we're going back to France at the end of this?" I asked Cecile as she buckled in the seat belts on the car seats. I pictured our quiet, empty third floor apartment with the bakery around the corner and the Dijon bustle as shoppers went to Saturday morning market.

"Give me one reason why we shouldn't?" my wife challenged.

"Because here, we can keep looking," I replied.

We turned south back into Arizona. We had more land waiting. We had a coast to see. I lay on the accelerator to get us going on the next bracing morning in the desert.

- - -

The next two weeks offered an almost hourly taking away of breath. Savage natural spectacle waited at every marked exit across the national park-loaded Colorado Plateau. Despite the miles covered, we would still only see a fraction of the area.

After Monument Valley, we stayed a night in the nearby Glen Canyon Recreation Area known otherwise by the reservoir formed when the Bureau of Reclamation constructed a dam here in the 1960s to create Lake Powell. Glen Canyon featured the same colorful lines in the rock we'd seen in Monument Valley, though here they were more striking and in a way that made the layers of history more evident. I especially liked being reminded that the canyon was, in many sections, comprised of compressed sand dunes. Lines toward the bottom of the canyon, just above the surface of the lake, also showed how the water had dropped only recently. At the campground near the Wahweap Marina on Lake Powell, one of several inlets with a boat launch, stores and restaurants, we had views onto the cliffsides and clean modern looking sites within walking-distance of a small beach. The day was one of the hottest yet.

From there we found Bryce Canyon, where the air cooled and the low, scrubby vegetation grew into pine forests as we climbed in elevation. The deep evergreen sprouted from the red desert whose rocks gradually shone a brilliant orange.

Something called a hoodoo rose from this topography. In Bryce, wind and water have eroded the first big "step" in such a way to carve detail-oriented towers and pillars, hoodoos, which according to the Bryce Canyon pamphlet handed to us at the park entrance, meant "to cast a spell." I came to prefer the name fairy chimney, but whatever the nomenclature, these formations unique to Bryce Canyon looked as though they were crafted by nature chiefly for the purpose of attracting onlookers. And it had worked. Three ranger-operated booths marked the entrance and all had lines over twenty vehicles deep.

Once inside, it was only a short turn-off from the road until we were able to stand at the edge of the Bryce Amphitheater. Focusing one's eyes on the hoodoos individually, they look like columns or minarets on the world's most elaborate castle. A well-known hoodoo, named Thor's Hammer, could even be a warning. But if we pull back to take in the entire scene at once, the orange, red and white points by the thousands become flames of a forest fire that hardened there into stone, a glorious construction that marks the high north end of the slope descending southward along the Grand Staircase until it drops finally into the Grand Canyon.

Beyond the geology, I also learned that Bryce has another visual distinction. Due to a combination of altitude, remote location and low levels of air pollution, the sky over this park is one of the most ideal in the country for stargazing. As we roasted marshmallows on the campfire after dinner with the girls in the Sunset Campground, daylight disappeared and thousands of shining stars poked out of the darkness through the tops of the pines.

It led me to the decision to spend the night, for the first time, outside the camper. We tucked the girls in and Cecile nodded off shortly after, retiring to the back bed. I proceeded to lay down the tarp on the most level spot I could find. I inflated a thermarest and unrolled my sleeping bag over it. I also pulled on another sweater and zipped up my fleece jacket. As the night fully descended over the woods, the temperature plummeted like we'd entered another season. It was mid-July in the Southwest, but Bryce Canyon left me shivering.

Despite the cold, I couldn't let the stars go. I crawled into the sleeping bag and pulled the drawstring of its polyurethane hood component over my head. The stellar night lights and the tall trees that reached for them were all I could see. The largest stars glowed like stage lights while others faded together into white clusters over the black tablet of space. The swath of the Milky Way, its boundaries easily traceable, hung superimposed over the brighter points in the sky. I held my eyes open. Later, I'd be left with the impression of dreaming without ever closing them. The constellations assumed the role of the inside of my eyelids and, for that night, the two became one in the same.

There is an idea referred to as the Attention Restoration Theory in a blog called Science Direct, the Journal of Environmental Psychology. In it, they point to a study by Marc Berman, John Jonides and Stephen Kaplan from Psychological Science positing that interaction with nature provides a marked improvement in a person's capacities for directed attention, working memory and overall cognitive function. This happens because nature is filled with inherently interesting stimuli that trigger our involuntary attention in, as the researchers say, "a modest way." The article states, "Because you can't help but stop and notice the reddish orange twilight sky – paying attention to the sunset doesn't take any extra work or cognitive control – our attentional circuits are able to refresh themselves. A walk in the woods is like a vacation for the prefrontal cortex."

They explain that the opposite is true of urban environments where we're forced to stay vigilant as we avoid being hit by a car while also ignoring superfluous stimuli like billboards or the passing parade of other pedestrians. Nature, lucky for us, is loaded with sensory experiences that we are drawn to, naturally. It replenishes our weary directed attention.

The study provides a scientific reaffirmation of something most outdoor types have long known. It doesn't require scientific analysis to understand that when you look at the stars in Bryce Canyon your brain is breathing an ancient sigh of relief.

I woke early the next morning to pale light and convivial birds. I was cold, my back was kinked on one side and I didn't want to bother changing the clothes I'd slept in so as not to reveal how badly I needed a shower. But breathing the pure air all night coupled with the reminder that a roof over your head was not a given necessity in one's life, was a full-blown rejuvenation.

Everyone inside our vehicle remained asleep. I got behind the wheel and pulled out at seven a.m. from our site. Few other campers had stirred; the main road through Bryce was deserted. In the dawn light coming through the pines, I passed mule deer grazing in the forest grass. My directed attention continued to be spoiled.

Within minutes, Julie and Louise woke, hooting at the discovery that their day began with a kind of carnival ride in their beds. Having them in the cabover while driving was not what you would technically call legal nor safe. But for this morning stretch I'd broken the rules.

Outside the boundary of the national park, we pulled into the lot of Ruby's Inn horse ranch where Cecile and Julie had an appointment with some cowboys and horses. Julie began a new wave of hooting and jumping in place when she realized this was the morning of her horseback ride we'd reserved.

We tried to downplay it in Louise's presence. The ranch hands told us Louise was too small to ride, even if accompanied by an adult. So Cecile hopped out quickly with Julie, trying not to spread more enthusiasm until her little sister was out of earshot. The leather chap-clad guides presented them with their morning ride, a large dark brown horse named Big Mack. Cecile saddled up first and Julie was hoisted into the space in front, where she grabbed the reins. They rode off into the sunrise, both Cecile and Julie wearing a smile from ear-to-ear.

"*Moi aussi*, horse," Louise called out, standing on the bottom rung of the wooden fence of the corral.

Me too, she said. It was the refrain of younger siblings everywhere. She looked up at me, waiting to be told which steed she'd be galloping away on.

"Hey Louise," I pointed across the street to a diner, "for the cowgirls who stayed back, they have waffles."

After the rough riders returned, we headed south out of Bryce. Julie and Cecile talked for the rest of the day about what they'd seen and how it would be so much better if we could continue the rest of our trip on horseback.

"And trade in this stallion?" I asked, stroking our dashboard.

"You are right. I don't want to say goodbye to the Cruiser Royale." Cecile conceded. "Hey, would you like me to drive for awhile?" Cecile asked, game to be directing our motion after taking the reins that morning. She hadn't yet touched the wheel on the trip. From the beginning, I had assumed the conventional role of family driver. A break- perhaps even a nap- sounded nice for once.

At a rest stop, Cecile took the driver's side, adjusted the bucket seat, selected her own music and merged back onto the highway. We descended out of the mountain climate and back into the hot, dry summer. In my half-waking state, I heard Cecile say we could save gas by moving in neutral downhill. Suddenly, we lurched forward.

"What's going on?!" I jerked alert. The engine petered out. All the instrument panel dials swung to zero. Cecile veered the camper onto the shoulder.

"I don't know!" Cecile answered.

"The thing just broke down?! It just stopped, like that?" We slowly rolled onto the side of the road to a dead stop.

"While I was trying to put it in neutral, I might have…" Cecile explained.

"What?"

"I might have gone into reverse instead."

"Okay, give me the keys."

"No panic please."

Thus ended Cecile's stint as a driver. It sounded like a bad stereotype, but Cecile belonged in the passenger seat. The gender roles arched traditional again. I became still more possessive of the helm of our camper. So I insisted on a switch, back to our trusted posts. I turned the ignition and the engine started up once more, without a sputter. Now I knew what happened to a 19-foot vehicle when you threw it into reverse going 60 miles an hour.

"So everything is fine?" Cecile smirked sheepishly beside me.

"Maybe you should stick to horses."

"And you need to stick to relaxing. If we break down, we break down. Who cares?"

I raised my hand. "Me."

"Remember we're on vacation."

- - -

We had one more canyon to see. Rumors claimed it was grand.

The road to the South Rim of the Grand Canyon from the east is dead and sun-bleached. More dusty Navajo jewelry stands lined the road. Then, after several miles, the ravine to the right carved by a Colorado River tributary deepens.

On the approach, bristly underbrush blocked all views. Signs for the scenic viewpoints appeared. I suggested we wait until the main overlook with the optimal view so we could let the full effect of the Grand Canyon hit us all at once. We wouldn't make it to Grand Canyon West, the new hot spot of the monument thanks to the 70-foot glass walkway called the Skywalk, the highest man-made structure in the world where visitors can test their vertigo over the portion of the canyon that funnels into Lake Mead. We also would only be spending a few hours at this world-famous monument, so had no time to waste.

As we skirted the South Rim, finding the principal overlook was trickier than it was supposed to be. We stopped to inspect the detailed park service map. Only once we looked beyond the arteries of bus lines around the park, as complicated as any city mass transit system, could we make out the key access points. We parked along the road after the Yavapai lookout and set out for a path we found through the trees. We came upon a paved walkway that held a steady stream of hushed tourists and hikers. To get an idea of where we were, I glanced over the low stone wall.

From that ledge, I saw two billion years of earth cracked open beneath our feet.

I'd sometimes envision the world from Louise's perspective. Her eye level was somewhere at the bottom of my pants pocket. On a queen-sized bed, her whole body, with her tiny toes pointed, stretched to a little over a third of the bed's length. I tried to imagine sleeping in a bed three times as long as I was or having to crane your neck skyward to talk with the gigantic people in your life.

So what did this mile-down hole look like to her? The stone wall along the walkway came up to her chin. She stood there for a moment with the rest of us, her pink floppy hat blocking out the roasting sun.

The thin ribbon of the Colorado River meandered through the canyon floor. Above it stood hundreds of smaller plateaus, mesas, buttes and "temples" within the canyon, each of various colors between dark brown, tan, yellow, white, pink, red and purple and each representing another epoch in the planet's history. The North Rim was ghosted out white in the haze but otherwise seemed to be just in front of us. But, drawing a straight line through the sky, the other side of the canyon at that point was actually ten miles away.

The land had taken on these kind of proportions and all the wee visitors that had made the pilgrimage here, whether they'd taken air-conditioned buses or hiked to the bottom with gallons of water strapped to their back, were like grains of sand that dusted the surface of the rocks.

I lingered by the precipice. Despite the hype generated by the five million plus who visit the park every year, despite the overcrowded luxury lodges and overpriced food in the Grand Canyon Village, the overflow parking lots full of charter buses and the racks of Grand Canyon-branded goods at the gift shop, the sight didn't fail to be a revelation when we stepped up to it.

The world, operating here on its own, proper scale, has been pulled apart. From the safety of this rim, we could pretend that we ourselves were as epic.

Louise and I stretched our arms out as the wind picked up blowing across the top of the expanse.

Catchy Names for Geologic Layers in the Grand Canyon
* Hermit Shale
* Bright Angel Shale
* Tonto Group
* Muav Formation
* Cenozoic Lava
* Vishnu Basement

Things that Test Our So-Called "Fragile Kinship" with the Grand Canyon
 * the Grand Canyon IMAX adventure narrated by Robert Redford
* the wifi access at all points along the rim
* the five-dollar mineral water bottles at the lodge
* "Brighty"the Grand Canyon plush mule

* the courage bracelets available in Bear Claw, Kokopeli or Thunderbird
* the beef tenderloin with wild shrimp at the El Tovar lodge
* the abandoned Flintstones Bedrock Village south of the park
* me thinking I can encapsulate the Grand Canyon in a description based on an afternoon's visit and fathom any of its larger implications

We got onto one of the transit buses and toured the west end of the rim near a point called Hermit's Rest. The canyon showed off all new textures from this end. Before returning to the camper, we took one last view from Mather Point, named after Steven Mather, the first director of the National Park Service. Nearby, the only developed campground of the park held hikers preparing for trips to the bottom and more families like ours.

I wished I'd taken the time to reserve a spot here. But we had to shove on. We had family awaiting us in Flagstaff.

- - -

At the beginning of the summer, we all, my brother and parents and the four residents of our camper, had decided to convene in the Coconino Forest just south of Flagstaff where an old cabin, formerly used as a ranger fire station, was available to rent through park service. It wasn't a finely appointed lodge, but it had a kitchen and running water and room to sleep us all under one roof.

So my parents, in their own rented motorhome, and my brother in a car, met us out here on the road. We found each other in a parking lot in Flagstaff at the entrance to the forest road going toward the cabin.

"Well, bud!" my Dad called out from the driver's side window of his camper as I poked my head out of ours. Your father's face appearing in territory you've never set foot in before creates an immediate anchor on that particular patch of Earth. I hadn't been adrift this whole time.

From there, in a mini-convoy, we all jostled our way down the dirt road toward the cabin. My younger brother, Whit, drove ahead in his car. Soon, though he turned around and waved us to stop.

"Yeah, so the road's closed ahead," he said standing in the settling red dust we'd kicked up.

"The cabin's not for another ten miles," I said.

"Sounds like we can cross the cabin off the list then," he concluded.

We'd already paid for three nights. We all threw up our arms. I looked behind me where Cecile and the girls were pointing toward the woods. We were surrounded by ponderosa pines and a soft carpet of blue-green grass. Like many of the forests of the West, the trees were spaced far apart with no branches within arms' reach, so the environment seemed cleaner and fresher. In the distance, a meadow opened up.

"We could camp right here," Cecile suggested. We all paused on the new solution that should have been obvious. We found level ground in dry grass and parked our two campers beside one another. As we unfolded canvas chairs, we discovered a firepit with a stack of unused wood beside it. We'd come to the right place.

My mom had other supplies to unpack. She is someone who never misses the chance to celebrate a birthday. Despite her children and grandchildren scattered at various time zones across the globe, she always managed at least a card and a phone call and usually a gift. She often reminds friends when theirs was coming up, sometimes before they themselves have bothered to remember. I believe this had happened more than once with my Dad.

For my brother's 30th birthday, she'd brought along hats, streamers and a cake. That we were in a primitive camping spot beside an open meadow with no trace of other fellow human beings for miles, made little difference.

So once the blanket was spread and a fire started from gathered sticks and logs, we lit the candles on a cake and sang a happy birthday to Whit in a rendition that echoed through the undisturbed forest. In our late teens and twenties we always felt obliged to perform endless eye-rolls to her birthday fêting. But by now, I'd come to appreciate my mother's reliability and the unassailable sincerity of the birthday well wishes. Though I don't know if my brother was with me on this yet. As a test, my mom and his nieces sprayed him down with purple silly string.

Darkness like we'd not yet seen on this trip descended. The sky was slightly overcast so there was no visible light from the moon or stars and the remoteness of this location meant no other signs of other campers anywhere, no other flickering campfires in the distance and none of the occasional passing beam of other flashlights. The five of us circled around the flames and continued an uninterrupted flow of conversation like we were sitting in our old family den.

<u>Topics of Conversation Around the Fire with My Family</u>
* when Whit will settle down with someone now that he's thirty
* why he's not interested in that anytime soon
* how disappointing the new Indiana Jones movie was
* my Dad's over-serious tending of the fire
* how the Coconino Forest Service had screwed us
* how we should have planned to stay right here in the dispersed camping wilderness all along
* how I appeared to everyone else as I squatted for an emergency bathroom break over that log at the far end of the meadow
* whether other people spent this much time talking together about bathroom habits
* Cecile's patience with our family
* pronunciation of French words my parents were both working on
* why Anglophones can never master the difference between the "*u*" and "*ou*" French vowel sounds because something is wrong with our mouths
* where my sister was and what she must be up to at this very moment
* the next time we'd all get together again

The next morning, our two girl-shaped roosters woke the group. My mom was glad to have her usual morning eagerness matched by Julie and Louise. If it had been provisioned out, we could have stayed another night in the open forest site, but we voted to keep exploring.

We rejoined Highway 89A that wound south from Flagstaff to Sedona. It took us through Oak Creek Canyon where we plunked down at the Pine Flat campground, booked solid by late afternoon. The affable campground hosts, a young couple dressed in their army green Red Rock Ranger District uniforms, sold us firewood. They also made sure to tell us about the glories of their natural spring water.

"It's artesian spring water," the ranger told us like it was unclaimed gold in the hills. "People come from miles for it," he explained. According to him, the natural springs of the canyon pump out some of the purest mountain spring water in the country. For time immemorial, the Native American tribes of the area have believed that the water contains healing powers. The Pine Flat campground had multiple spigots that tapped into the spring, one along the shoulder of the canyon road that was never without a line of cars beside it. Water-seekers filled bottles or large water cooler jugs that were then heaved back into their trunk.

The ranger was right that the water tasted pure. We had sampled a variety of potable water in the past month. We'd become water connoisseurs. The water at Ute Lake in New Mexico, for example, had come out of a rusty pipe in the ground and had given us indigestion. The water from the hand-cranked pumps in the southern Virginia campground came out warm as bathwater. In Oklahoma, the only water available was from the hose that was meant to hook into the RV. In questionable cases like these we didn't let the girls drink the water, using the store-bought jugs kept on hand. But Cecile and I always took a chance hydrating from the local supply.

The water at Oak Creek made a good case for being the coolest and most refreshing I'd tried so far, cool mineral water shooting straight out of the depths of an untouched peak. The stone column that held the spigot near our campsite was emblazoned with a plaque that certified this H2O as artesian. We topped off every bottle, jug and holding tank we had with these precious commodity. Given recent news of the dangerously-depleted water supply in Phoenix, the fifth most populated city in the nation that receives less than nine inches of rain a year, we could see why people weren't taking the Arizona groundwater for granted.

Wet is worshipped further a few miles south of the campground. Slide Rock State Park is a recreation area where Oak Creek flows over slippery rocks and shallow pools making for a natural waterslide. Cecile, Whit and I passed the afternoon there with the girls. It was just like the Sliding Rock we'd splashed around in with my sister in North Carolina but more expansive, less choked with vegetation and with gentler sloping rocks. The creek swirled into rapids in some places and funneled into chutes in others and, at key bends, deepened into tranquil pools. The waters couldn't have been designed better. And they washed over visitors of all shapes and sizes. I spent much of the afternoon observing.

Types You'll Spot at Any Popular Natural Waterslide or Wading Pool
* pre-teen boys who seem to be part-amphibian
* toddlers who think this is the best bathtub ever
* a teenage boy in shorts past his knees slipping on rocks and pretending not to be experiencing blinding white pain in his backbone
* a Christian youth group cheering too loudly as one of their members takes the plunge down the rock slide
* passing hikers who've stopped to cool off looking like they haven't seen water in days
* guys off to the side trying to hide that they're smoking a joint
* an older man who seems to using the river for bathing and personal hygiene
* an infant over-lathered with sunscreen and saddled with sunglasses and a sun hat whom the mother lets briefly touch a puddle
* girls in bikinis sunbathing on rocks acting like they don't want to be splashed by the guys they came with
* a middle-aged woman who is cautious at first but then turns out to be a graceful swimmer

There were also two little girls, one who took her time getting into the water while she pointed out minnows along the banks and another who'd already plopped into the water and sat submerged chest-high, dribbling streambed pebbles through her fingers. Nearby, their parents and uncle watched. As I've come to see as my duty, I stopped watching and eased into the brisk water, letting it push me down the river with everything else.

We stayed the next night in Sedona. Nestled into a stunning red rock area, Sedona has come to acquire a reputation as hippie. I've heard the term "New Age Disneyland" applied. On the outskirts of the town are several spots in the ground where one can evidently find "vortexes", supposed points in the earth from which a mystical energy force flows. Tour packages are based around these vortexes.

But the first thing you notice upon arriving to Sedona, after you come out of the deep red beauty of the surrounding mesas, is that it seems to consist almost entirely of gated resort communities. George Clooney has a house somewhere in these hills. As does the then desperately-seeking-White House, John McCain. I wondered which vortex they'd chosen. Sedona's rising popularity is betrayed by the subdued look of all the development. A Sedona law prohibits the use of any other color for commercial establishments beside tan, teal or the same red as the buttes towering in the distance behind them. It's a welcome change from the sometimes eyesore juxtaposition of styles and colors in most growing cities. Though, in the end, what does it actually change if the arches of McDonalds are teal green instead of yellow? And how about the mysticism in the $39.99 Buddha statue with gurgling Zen mini-fountain?

Still, here people were making a comfortable living doing and creating what they loved. And how could one argue with anything promoting optimism and peace, even if the message was delivered with it a tinge of self-importance and was simplified into something tourist-friendly?

And the community benefited. The Mexican arts and craft village, called Tlaquepaque, featured artisans selling traditional jewelry, clothing, music, sculpture and paintings. They were genuinely devoted to their art and the village, even if balanced just on the borderline of looking like Epcot Center's Mexico.

The town also gave nods to its cowboy heritage. We ate lunch that day at the Cowboy Club Grille, where the ribeye special is listed in a special section on the menu surrounded by smoking six-shooters. It also includes fried strips of Nopalitas cactus and skewered rattlesnake meat. The décor is festive, but classy enough that you don't feel like you're at Sizzler. On the far wall, a colorful Western mural celebrates the joint as the birthplace of Cowboy Artists of America. With the seven of us at a long table together all sharing in the rattlesnake sampler under low blue and red lights, this would be one of the finer lunches I'd had in recent memory.

We took advantage of my parents' presence by going out with my brother in search of a bar. Nightlife being a more revealing litmus test of a community, we needed the unvarnished take on Sedona. As it happened, we were forced to drive five miles out of the city center before finding a bar not connected to a resort that was, at the same time, open past ten o'clock. The bar we finally did discover had a handful of patrons and a large hall of empty seats.

From the nightlife of Sedona, one got the impression the cowboys had given up wetting their whistle with whiskey into the wee hours in favor of hot stone massages and afternoon rounds of golf.

Before we left Arizona altogether, we brought the camper to Big O Tires for servicing. It was time to change the oil and top off fluids and tanks and carburetors and overflow rack and pinion steering columns and check the gaskets and sprockets and valves and flux capacitors and dynamo fuel cell defibrillators. Though I liked to think I'd learned a thing or two about the inner-workings of the RV because I'd bothered to research the difference between an inverter and a converter, I knew embarrassingly little about anything under the hood.

This was evidenced by the maintenance that I performed which involved changing the duct tape on the air conditioning cover and repositioning the bungee cord that held it down as a backup. These makeshift features had become essential vehicle parts. Meanwhile, inside the cabin things were worse for their wear.

Other Things No Longer Working Inside the Camper
* the top drawer under the sink permanently jammed shut
* the propane intake
* the refrigerator (by extension)
* the rubber seal around the back windows that prevented water from leaking in
* the screens on the cabover area
* the left headlight (still)

The mechanic returned the keys to me impressed.

"You came all the way from New York?"
"Yep."
"And that's a rental?"
"That's right. How did everything look?"
"Pretty good. Considering."
I wasn't sure what we were considering, but I assumed he'd noticed the duct tape. He'd probably expected something similarly ramshackle in the transmission. The camper engine, however, hadn't let us down.

- - -

We shook off dust on 40 West. We kept neck and neck with the trucks after Flagstaff, the crush of deliveries- goods, visitors or residents returning- all chugging toward Los Angeles. The traffic flowed until we turned north toward Nevada.

There, we met another checkpoint. We were asked to pull over again. This one came at the request of officers from the Department of Homeland Security. They wore approximately the same hardened blank on their faces as the border patrol in New Mexico, though with the hint of a more heroic, and therefore still less contestable, purpose. We were not potential illegal immigrants here, but rather potential terrorists.

We were a mother and father with two young daughters and a mobile home full of camping supplies sporting New York plates. It had been a nice trip so far, but now it was time to blow up the Hoover Dam. I told Louise to hide her Kalashnikov.

I joke about it here because I couldn't as the officers inspected our camper. I joke about it to while away the absurdity that we are now living in the world where my overblown illustration is within the limits of possibility. Our family, being frequent plane travelers, had learned to take life with these threats as a given, like everyone else. We tried to be cooperative and wary and continue as if things were normal.

It was up for debate whether the security checkpoint only encouraged otherwise nonexistent thoughts about what would happen if you destroyed the world's second largest hydroelectric dam, taking away power from most of the Southwest and unleashing Lake Mead onto Las Vegas. It was best just to hum something tunelessly until you could proceed, pretending things were as you once remembered them.

Once our vehicle inspection was finished, the officer cracked a smile. He lowered his sunglasses and gave Louise a pinch on the cheek. She chuckled like he could have been her grandfather. The officer was trying to move on too, which we could count as its own larger act of heroism.

After the checkpoint, traffic oozed along the Hoover Dam. We got a prolonged glimpse of the concrete engineering miracle as we inched along its narrow switchbacks. The road could no longer handle the traffic, especially the trucks which looked at any moment like they could tip over the guardrail and tumble down the side of the dam. But a bypass was on the way. Construction had been completed already on a set of support columns on either side of the gorge waiting to hold the arches of the coming bridge.

We passed the casino towns of Boulder City and Henderson until a hazy view of brighter lights beyond our windshield. We found Las Vegas. We hadn't come west for the nature alone.

Simone de Beauvoir came this way too. She commented on this city in the desert and the national zeitgeist it distilled: "Tourism has a privileged character in America: it doesn't cut you off from the country it's revealing to you; on the contrary, it's a way of entering it."

Las Vegas becomes a truer portal into the American psyche every year. In its monument to artifice, it is the most frank about its actual purpose and the unashamed desires of its visitors. So it is also one of the few cities in the country not attempting to be something it is not since, sprung up amidst nowhere, it was never supposed to exist in the first place. It runs wholly on borrowed time.

From the highway, rising before us, came a space needle, the New York City skyline and a black Egyptian pyramid beside a tall white hotel with shimmering gold windows. The last one was the Mandalay Bay, where we'd booked a room for two nights.

We rolled down the Strip and got a close view of the clowns at Circus Circus, the pirate ships at Treasure Island, the white steps of the Venetian and then Paris Las Vegas where the lights of the Eiffel Tower rose above the line of palm trees. At the tower's base, a streetside café offered *croque monsieur* and *fruit des mers* while the white-shirted serveurs ferried trays of kir to the people seated at the small round outdoor tables.

What amazed me was the ability of the tourists to buy the conceit so thoroughly that they themselves started to look like Parisians. Maybe some of them were. It also made me think that one day we could open a Las Vegas-themed hotel somewhere on the Champs Elysée or on Place Darcy in Dijon. The French could have their pictures taken beside statues of Frank Sinatra and Dean Martin before they entered a faux-Sands hotel and casino. People would come from kilometers.

But instead we were in this faux fakeness. We parked adjacent to our hotel, in the convention center overflow parking area at the very end of the all the glitz where the hotels turned long-stay and seedy.

The mountains that rimmed Las Vegas turned purple in the desert dusk. The nightlife wattage took over. People trotted out of the hotel in their snazzier evening wear carrying pink souvenir shooter glasses, feeling lucky.

I pulled out slightly decent pants and Cecile, a skirt, both items that hadn't been touched since we folded them into our suitcase back in Dijon. We all marched toward the Mandalay Bay, the 21st century tropical palace before us. We followed the entrance signs. The only way toward the front doors was in a car that, according to the sign, would be valet parked. We walked anyway, up a car ramp as taxis and limos whooshed by. Two Mandalay Bay employees told us we shouldn't be walking here. I was tempted to ask if we should hail a cab from the curb to get inside the hotel. They gave us elaborate directions that took us to the lower level entrance and elevator. There, we finally broke into the casino resort fortress.

The theme of the Mandalay Bay is more vague than some of the others. It is a Southeast Asian paradise, Thailand or Cambodia or Bali, but with enough non-specificity that thoughts don't drift to land mines, tsunamis or European colonialism. The gleaming marble lobby in gold and green tones had sky-high ceilings and, in the center, an immense tropical fish aquarium. The slight scent of lemons wafted from somewhere, giving the impression, along with all the potted greenery, of still being outside.

But beyond the lobby the calm exploded into a sensory blitz. We stood before the casino's gaming pit, ringing with the manic symphony of a million tiny pings and clangs lit to flashing yellows and reds that induced a near-instant disorientation in each of us. Julie took a single step down toward this area where minors were not permitted and intoned, "*Maman, c'est beau.*"

"Okay, we need to get out of here," I hurried everyone along.

The room had the same effect on all four of us. We had splurged on a small suite with a separate room where we could watch t.v. at night without disturbing the girls. Upon entering the room, I realized access to television wouldn't be a problem, as the suite had three plasma screens, including one over the sink in the bathroom, in case you needed a diversion during the five minutes spent brushing your teeth. I lost interest in the t.v. when seeing the marble bathtub and shower, an unimaginable luxury after weeks in communal campground showers. While I rifled through the complimentary bottles of soap and aftershave, Cecile and the girls opened the curtains onto the view. The Luxor shot a beam of light toward the sky in front of the Camelot spires of the Excalibur hotel. The MGM Grand cast a green and gold glow up the street toward the rest of this adult playground approaching peak exuberance.

It was going to be hard to get the girls to return to any campground ever again.

The next day saw nonstop, wallet-vaporizing fun for the whole family. We started that morning at the hotel's shark reef, followed, without a hint of trepidation, by a dip in the outdoor wave pool and a lazy tropical river.

During naptime, Cecile and I took one turn each in the casino. I decided it best not to throw the remaining trip funds on anything more than video poker. The machines didn't take coins anymore, nor did they spew money when you cashed out. The casino used a system of credits printed out on a receipt. They'd added another trip if you want to collect your hard cash, making it infinitely simpler to feed your credit receipt back to the slots and other machines. Nothing but small laserjet printed digits got bigger or smaller. Cecile or I returned from our brief separate gambling adventures, reporting a number in the negative just shy of the truth.

One of my favorite things to do in Las Vegas was to read about restaurants I couldn't afford. Mandalay Bay alone has twenty-two different restaurants. One of the highest-rated is called Aureole, known for its wine list. It has a sleek and mysterious white façade, like the entrance to the waiting room of heaven. Inside, the restaurant houses a 42-

foot temperature-controlled wine tower that contains close to ten thousand bottles of wine. Not stopping there, the Plexiglas tower also includes bungee jumping "wine angels," trained acrobats who fly up and down inside the tower in less than ten seconds to deliver your evening's selection. Of course, we never dined there. But it is the continued genius of Las Vegas to introduce to the world terms like "wine angels."

It is the further genius of the town that it manages to make the large majority of its workers, from the dealers to gift shop cashiers to the maid service, seem genuinely happy to be doing their jobs. As the hostess at the buffet ran down prices, she said children under 3 eat free. When we truthfully responded that Julie was 4, she replied "What, you say she's 3?" She smiled knowingly at us as we paid for only two meals.

We also ran into a woman trying to sell condo visitation sessions. She proposed we sit through two hours of a lecture about an exciting new property still nearing completion in exchange for gambling chips and an extra hotel night at a reduced rate. She leveled with us when we expressed our disinterest. "You don't have to buy a thing, but I get credit for it if you show. C'mon, you don't even want to help me out?" she laughed, sounding like an old friend.

The saleswoman pushed units in something called CityCenter, a high-rise residential condo development in the dead center of the Strip. She gestured to a mock-up of the finished structure, proclaiming CityCenter as a visionary "city-within-a-city" that would transform the Strip into a major urban center.

To me, the idea did nothing but let the gas out of the high times of Vegas. Would it still be Sin City as a bustling residential urban center? And unless your name is Louie Anderson, does anybody really want to live on the Las Vegas Strip? Aren't all the people from all over the world coming to Vegas for the extended bender weekend, where you could just be everything but yourself for a few days and then return to your life elsewhere, letting what happened there stay there, as the saying goes? To me, an oversized complex for timesharers and condo-dwellers would significantly choke the worldwide draw. It even knocked the unreal nature of Vegas down a few notches toward something more staid and practical. It was a little disappointing to see Vegas, the one city you expected never would, in the processing of growing up.

In the year following our visit, the CityCenter project had became plagued with various investor and real estate disputes. The tourism that de Beauvoir spoke of, that provided an entrance to the country, continued as before. The city had remained emblematic, here in the form of a stalled and vastly over-budget behemoth work-in-progress that had plenty of space left to fill and needed desperately for people to buy in.

We said sorry and goodbye to the sincere saleslady and the next day left town on a long road toward the Sierra Nevada Mountains. I didn't know when I'd ever have reason to return, but if I did things would probably be changed once again.

Every few years, people proclaim anew the glory days of Las Vegas to be over. But Vegas would continue to provoke the same giddiness and disbelief. Pleasure-seekers would keep coming to make something happen here that would always stay here, as the expression went. Tourists would continue to visit to say they've seen the Eiffel Tower. Las Vegas just may sustain itself, despite its improbability, despite the borrowed time on which it may live. For now, we place faith in wine angels.

- - -

You haven't really arrived until you've let Andrew McCarthy rack up debt on your Blockbuster card.
So I told myself a long time ago after making a life for myself in Los Angeles, California. It was long enough ago that I can relive it with a genuine fondness, but not long enough to feel casual about seeing it as a "time."
I'd crossed the country after college to live in this LA. The city held my crowded visions of movies as products of an innocent, worldwide imagination. In the case of the employer to whom I'd first hitched my star, I'd settled for t.v. movies and a smaller niche. Upon landing this first real job of my life, I awarded myself an early E for effort, and for entertainment.
Among household names in this time I worked as an assistant to the office assistant of a producer were "Blockbuster", "videocassette" and "the end-of-millennium." "Andrew McCarthy" was ahead of the rest on gradually fading away. He was set to star in a 10 o' clock network original playing a single father fighting for custody of his adopted child after his wife's sudden death.

I calculated he owed me thirty dollars. The production company had rented the movies of McCarthy's costar, for his own research purposes. I'd be sent on the task of obtaining them and had used petty cash, but my own card still got strapped with the late fees. I'd mentioned this to my boss, the producer. But he hardly noticed when I spoke. I was only the runner, the gopher, the schlepper, but I saw myself as helping to work the gears and cogs behind the silver screen. I was grinding out the tinsel. Having a tether to an eighties brat packer was something I could own.

But my boss was concerned with the medium cup of chocolate vanilla frozen yogurt I was to drop off, beside, but not on, his desk. He had informed me the first day he was classic OCD. He ate only frozen yogurt for lunch and only with a plastic spoon. His assistant had warned me never, ever to make the mistake of providing a metal one.

I remember entering his office and getting a glimpse of the kingdom below, looking onto the bend in Sunset Boulevard where the street changed from billboards and nightclubs of famous celebrity overdoses and widened to the overwatered greenery of homes waiting for the occupants to return. I set down the frozen yogurt and picked up a script to be delivered to Andrew McCarthy. I dashed out of the office and back to my car, motoring up Coldwater Canyon to hand Mr. McCarthy his script, only to be disappointed when I was greeted at the door by an unknown hanger-on friend, who thanked me sincerely and promised me he'd see that Andrew got this.

I waited for a minute in the driveway under a canopy of broad leaves that I took for banana trees. Under its shade,

I hoped something else might happen. But it was only autumn.

Because these were moments where things only *almost* did happen, moments that I'd later realize were possibly nothing, or else opportunities with the potential to change my future, if only I had the small legend in the corner of my daydreaming to be able to tell the difference.

I drove home in the evening, closing the dog-eared pages of my Thomas Bros map of LA County and tossing it in the backseat beside a copy of my own newly-bradded screenplay that still sought a place to be dropped off. I headed back toward my apartment in the other direction on Sunset willing myself to be bolder. I shuffled through personas.

After six, the air hung hazed a reddish orange by the actual sunset in my rearview mirror. The streets had cooled. I drove by a homeless man dressed in a white robe like a prizefighter, then the Viper Room and, farther down, a billboard of a woman named Angelyne in a pink Corvette, blonde hair and monumental boobs, who seemed to be some kind of street marketing genius having already captured so many hearts and minds with nothing for sale but herself.

I realized I should have dropped off my own script that afternoon. Or maybe Andrew McCarthy was not right for the role of the lead. Either way, the myriad formatting errors and core structural flaws would be cleaned up during the notes meetings I was bound to have once the thing was bought. Andrew would be the kind of guy who understood what was essential. The idea of just handing it over to him without a word could work. My delusions, I assumed, boded well for my future success in the industry.

I continued on as the traffic got lighter. I decided to dip three blocks south of my apartment by the Formosa Café.

At a lonely corner, its eerie green lights glowed over the striped black and white awnings that could never have come from this half of the century. It looked like Lana Turner could be in there, or the actress who played Lana Turner in L.A. Confidential where Guy Pearce tosses a drink in her face having mistaken her for a hooker. I'd seen the movie the weekend before and it had reaffirmed my belief that, in the west, they didn't build over sagging remnants of the past, they just left them abandoned to drop into the present desert and noir.

I reminded myself then that I'd been born in a hospital in Pasadena. I'd spent the first year of my life there, during a time when my parents lived above a garage. I like to think I remember the place in my bones, and not just in photos. It meant this roiling southland was home.

Not long after, my boss informed me that his nephew wanted his job back, the job that I happened to currently hold. He was sorry, but there was no other way to do it, and he couldn't say no to family. I'd figured something like this was coming.

As one of the first orders of business, I placed a random Blockbuster receipt in the petty cash drawer and helped myself to triple the amount listed. Andrew McCarthy for all I know never returned the rentals and enjoys them to this day.

Afterward, I temped and took strange jobs for a year. I met more people and happened upon more flashed moments of beauty that I'd never find anywhere else. I let the place seep back in, until eventually moving to San Francisco to follow a larger hysteria in the business of videogames.

But the day I left that office I'd begun to box up the trappings of a business and the parts that didn't accommodate an overthinker like me. I eulogized all the things that never came to fruition. I kept those that looked like a story. I blamed the movies for ingraining in me this need for closure. Though it may have been an unsatisfying one, it was an end for all parties just the same.

I stayed dazzled. My delusions remained intact. I had people to entertain elsewhere. My Blockbuster card still reflects the back charges.

Sometimes, despite the complicated fondness for Los Angeles, I don't want to relive these memories. Other times I always do. I never really shook my fascination with this city and with the movies, two entities which I considered interchangeable. And because the county was my birthplace, I never shook the movies from their hallowed space lodged in my id either. I would forever see my world, wherever I roamed, as cinematic. As in a movie, I like to think it was because I was born here. I have backstory in Los Angeles county.

So we didn't take the camper to L.A. I stayed away, remembering that it, more than most other locales, had a persistent ability to be perceived as something it was not.

The Los Angeles of my infant memory and then later of the melodramatic college graduate would be more useful to me. I couldn't go back to find that none of it matched the gauzy daydream. I couldn't go back to remind myself what was once becoming. Plus, I didn't have my old script with me. Nor the Blockbuster card.

Cecile, meanwhile, had another, related fantasy I needed to talk her out of - Disneyland.

I wanted to skip it too, but my reason wasn't so ambiguous or conflicted. I presented this case to Cecile.

Reasons Not to Visit Disneyland
* lines
* heat
* cheapest hotel within walking distance of park $350 a night
* admission prices $50 a head , taxes not included
* lines to get a Fast Pass
* reports of the California park falling into disrepair
* because one bender of conspicuous consumption in a place where the simulation had overtaken that being simulated was enough
* because once my kids saw Frontierland they may never again stop to read historic plaques about homesteaders and gold rushers.
* lines standing with Fast Pass in hand
* read that the ideal ages to take full advantage of a Disney visit are between 5 and 9, meaning we had time
* because the Haunted Mansion ride still scared me slightly
* lines to get Cinderella's autograph

* needed to preserve whatever modest amount of credibility I had with literary types, free-thinkers, weirdos and communists among whom I liked to be able to still feel partially accepted
* worried that a visit would be a final nail in the coffin of my carefree early adulthood and the next step was white sneakers, tucked T-shirts and a minivan

Cecile eventually came around to my side of the argument. We angled north, away from Los Angeles, away from Anaheim, away from the exalted dreams. I could feel the slight tingle of the stardust drifting in through the open window, as we escaped in the other direction, saving Southern California for another journey.

We drove along the northern edge of the Mojave Desert. As our rental agreement asked, we bypassed Death Valley. Nonetheless, the camper strained under the air conditioning on high-blast until we reached the suburban mecca of Bakersfield, where the landscape rippled and we pointed ourselves toward higher altitudes.

The hills gleamed as golden as the state nickname. We drove into greener pastures and through the fertile fields of the San Joaquin Valley, "the nation's salad bowl" so called because of the wealth of fruit and vegetables grown there. Rows of planted crops and ripening orchards stretched to the distant mountain ridges, at almost every mile marker from Bakersfield to the Sequoia National Forest, the latter being the point we were aiming for that day.

The San Joaquin Valley, or Central Valley, is one of the poorest parts of the state, but also the area that generations of outsiders had struggled to reach, whether the "Okies" leaving the Midwest or migrant workers from south of the border. There had been countless broken backs and hands worn to the bone in the crop rows we passed. As the sun set and the moon brightened, the sky over the hills turned rosy. The combines and the field hands disappeared, while extensive sprinkler tubing kept the soil drenched.

    We pulled into a nondescript campground called The Lemon Grove in Three Rivers, California. Other than light at the entrance, the facility was shrouded almost completely in darkness. We dropped the camping fee into the night box and checked the laminated map for available sites. Around us, we heard the sound of chirping crickets, a sprinkler tsking and a dog barking and rattling a chain we hoped was well-attached. In the pitch black, we found our pull-through site. Though we couldn't see much else, we could make out the shapes of the others in what must have been an RV-only park.

    We ate dinner by the beam of our flashlights, still on Vegas time and Vegas comforts and me with my ghostly visions of L.A. flickering somewhere on the southern horizon. We said goodnight to the waxing moon and its faint white light above us and curled up into our beds. It felt safe to be in the middle of nowhere again. We had absolutely nothing here to entertain us.

SAVE FOR FIREFLIES

- - -

The Sequoia National Park opened, as the second official national park in the nation, over 120 years ago. The trees of its forest had grown there for 3,000.

The biggest one had since been given the name General Sherman. This tree is not just the largest in the park, or the state or even only the tallest, broadest tree in the world. General Sherman is one of the largest things alive on our planet. It stands at 275 feet tall with a 103-foot circumference at its base, covered in a layer of bark a foot thick. Burl knots on its trunk loom larger than an SUV. In its three-millenia of life, the tree has seen a lot.

Things the Sequoias Have Weathered
*high elevation wind
*ice
*fire
* burrowing insects
*bears
*the Mono tribe settlements
*French fur trappers
*tourists driving and stalling their Model Ts
*John Muir and Teddy Roosevelt camping out at their base in an overnight meeting about federal park preservation
*an attempt by the Disney corporation to turn the area into a ski resort
*receiving names like "General Sherman" and "The Sentinel"
*smog

*the running of coaxal cables up to the visitor center
*the Bush Administration passing a law allowing guns in national parks
*a Franco-American family posing for a relatively hurried digital picture

We had trouble taking it all in, the history and the living thing itself. Only from a distance can you even begin to capture the whole prehistoric entity inside a camera lens. As before in the face of such natural spectacle, Julie and Louise were no longer the only people who looked like pipsqueaks.

The Sequoia forest still felt primeval and, despite the crowds that July, nature here hadn't been overrun yet. As we unloaded supplies, a deer expertly traversed the nearby creek, before leaping to the opposite bank and darting out of sight.

According to a pamphlet handed to us with our campground receipt, no soap or shampoo should be left inside a vehicle because the California black bear will rip off the doors and reduce your upholstery to ribbons. Likewise, no chewing gum or perfume should be left in the tent because the bear will come storming in to devour the occupants of the sleeping bags like fruit-roll ups. The ranger's paranoia for nature's big furry lugs came complete with photos of damaged cars.

I understood the urgency of preventing the wildlife from relying on human food and, for we intruders, the importance of not having our heads lopped off by the swipe of a bear paw. Still, after the first or second warning, the reminders of bear danger leaned toward overkill.

That night the moon came at us again, bigger than the sun as it rose above the forest. Its cool light shone down on the campground where the stout tree trunks divided its rays into a hundred slices. I stayed up later than usual, writing in my journal. I opened its pages and could almost read and write without any artificial bulb.

The full moonlight was neither light nor dark, nor was it the absence of either. I sat instead amidst shadows that revealed to me their bones. The red bark of the trees, the low brush along the stream and the soft, blank pages of my notebook chalked in white. Beyond our campsite, a rock outcropping marked a gap in the forest. I studied the open patch for a bear, scrounging for a place to lay his own weary moonstruck head.

I switched on the morning radio to a jazz and ragtime station. Al Jolson sang:

California, here I come!
Right back where I started from.
Where Bowers of flowers bloom in the spring.
Each morning at dawning, birdies sing an' everything.
A sunkissed miss said, "Don't be late" that's why I can hardly wait.
Open up that Golden Gate.
California here I come!

SAVE FOR FIREFLIES

We parted the dust in the flat town of Fresno. We pushed on through the sun-zapped Central Valley hills until Gilroy where we ramped north onto Highway 101. We'd be coming upon the San Francisco Bay Area on a Friday at 5:30 PM. We refilled the tank at a station outside San Jose, beside the shimmering silver flagship office of the Internet search engine Yahoo!. I suggested we go in and check to see if we had any new emails. But activity around the Yahoo! campus appeared deathly quiet, so I figured we shouldn't bother them.

From there, eight lanes funneled up and down the peninsula that finished at San Francisco. Or as the Chronicle columnist Herb Caen liked to refer to it, Baghdad-by-the-Bay (a name that would fall out of favor when the word Baghdad changed in connotation from "exotic" to "military quagmire").

I was partial to another nickname: Kookville. San Francisco was, and despite various evolutions still very much is, the city where all that has been daydreamed over, fantasized about or dismissed as too lofty and pie-in-the-sky elsewhere, here is turned into a daily way of life.

Cecile and I were, not so long ago, two such kooks.

- - -

In the first year of the new millennium, instant messaging was the fastest growing communication technology of all time. Cecile and I were among its then 60 million purported users. We worked at a public relations agency hyping Internet start-ups and video game companies, but cared only about the words we sent each other.

We sat in separate cubicles that shared a wall. Its segments fit together unevenly, leaving a narrow opening. We volleyed noiseless messages back and forth, five feet apart.

natm: fine i quit
cecilero: ok i will miss u
natm: you should come too
cecilero: where will u go?
natm: neptune or maybe mendocino
cecilero: i can see your left hand through the space
natm: i'm very serious

cecilero: this is typical

We were encouraged to use IM often, as it was the up-to-the-second way to communicate with clients. Exchanges were splintered, with multiple conversations blinking at once. Our VP, Pattie, sent missives with the fury of a Nasdaq ticker.

Pattier: heads up: out of pocket with ea til 4...
cecilero: pattie is writing to me
natm: no she's writing to me
cecilero: same time
natm: she's like a hydra
Pattier: need the % points from 99 and the final boiler on the release b4
cecilero: sorry i forgot to tell you but i am the hydra around here

natm: Thanks for your heads up, Pattie, I sent the finalized boilerplate this morning for your meeting with Electronic Arts. If they are not in your inbox, let me know and I will send them again.

Pattier: thx

In the evening, I commuted from the middle of the peninsula, north on highway 101 to the city. On Fridays, Cecile didn't have a car. She did have, however, a fiancée whom she would be marrying that summer back in their native France. He needed the car every Friday. So I would give Cecile a ride. I never asked many questions.

We joked after work. Other times, we listened as the radio filled the contained interior space between us, inching toward San Francisco on the road glutted with billboards of enchanted startups and cosmically revelatory business-to-business solutions. We passed the crowded airport and

Candlestick Park, with a new sponsored brand name every season. We spotted windsurfers and surprise lane departure collisions.

On a Friday in the Spring of that year, Cecile talked faster with the passenger window open.

"My fiancée is out of town."

"Ok."

"He's in New York all the weekend. But it's good because I have many things to plan. I don't have our guest list even. I don't want to think about it now."

"The wedding, you mean?"

"You know a thing- tomorrow I will have twenty-nine."

"Of what?"

"I mean to say tomorrow I will BE twenty-nine. My fiancée has something planned after he gets back. I think."

"Really? Your birthday's tomorrow? Huh…and here it is such a nice evening."

I pulled off at a gas station where I picked up a box of pink Little Debbie snack cakes and a six-pack of Anchor Steam. When I brought them back to the car, she looked touched about the cakes.

"You got these for my birthday?" she asked astounded. In her worn work shoes and her unruly blonde hair curling out of the clip she'd so carefully placed that morning, I wished she'd greeted these offerings with the appropriate eye-roll for the nimcompoop who'd brought them. But instead, she expressed gratitude. I had the urge to buy her a sapphire and diamond necklace just to measure further the innocent reaction. The little cakes made her smile, a natural beaming grin, all the way to the end of the peninsula.

I announced we'd be continuing further, across the bridge. We left the city and veered toward the Marin headlands. We parked along a wide shoulder of a curvy road. We stepped out of the car and into the tall grass of an overlook facing the city lights, brighter than the draining sunshine. A sneaky fog crept in below us. We ate the cakes and drank and watched as a cool white wall of cotton obscured the Golden Gate's red pylons and the twinkling cliffside of the fantasy metropolis we called home. Foghorns heaved out sighs from the water. I gave Cecile a sweatshirt from my trunk.

Our conversation shuttled from what her last year before thirty would look like to Pattie's inability to manage an office, to whether T.S. Eliot was American, to everything that could happen in California U.S.A. We didn't stop talking, tilting closer, until two in the morning when she nodded off against my shoulder. Her hair fell across my arm. To myself, I declared us a pair of star-crossed high school sweethearts too delicate to make moves. The foghorn bellowed two-notes back in a dirge to lost causes the world over.

We recrossed the bridge, nearly vacant at that hour. At the door to her apartment, I remembered to wish her a truly happy birthday.

"This," I said aloud, "this you should keep." I coasted home on a westbound street, having safely sent back Cecile. The fog lifted. The lights down Geary and an opening trapdoor out of a life staged for diminished expectations were then, and only for this transient moment, timed in my favor.

At the office the next morning, the residue of the sea and night made our endless ribbons of virtual dialogue actual.

natm: how are you feeling?
cecilero: have you finished the boilerplate yet?
natm: are you changing the subject?
cecilero: yes
natm: ok
cecilero: there is a thing you want to talk about?
natm: maybe
cecilero: it is fine, it is busy, crazzy

natm: it's spelled "crazzier"

cecilero: i feel bad.

The Internet charged ahead. Forty-five million people saw their hard drives hollowed-out by an e-mail bug named "I Love You." The cultural alarm bells said the prosperity couldn't last. The frenzy in our office was either jubilance or a death-rattle panic; it was hard to tell which one to pitch to journalists. We went with a story of two people getting married as their avatars in the fantasy realm of one of our clients' massively multiplayer online games. The press adored the angle. We had articles placed in magazines all over the country, sandwiched between dozens of pages of more ads than the publication's spine could handle. Cecile and I celebrated with the office over neon-colored cocktail shooters and catered chicken satay while we took turns wiping out on the half-pipe of the new skateboarding game on a beta PlayStation 2.

Pattie and three colleagues with matching Kate Spade bags wished us a good weekend. From there, another night freed itself of routine and probability. This one would be less harmless.

Again in my car, we zipped headlong away from the office and to the Pacific, assuming the right magic must be there. This time we tried farther down the coast. She wanted to know where I was going with this. I hadn't the foggiest.

Inside a state-run beach, we faced each other like we'd just hiked from opposite directions and met on this patch of sand. I pretended I had something I meant to say, but it had slipped my mind. She pretended she couldn't hear me over the waves. Visibility toward the horizon remained for mere minutes.

I kissed her after a lifetime of hesitation. When the wind picked up we scrambled to the car holding hands, where we pulled in closer. I tucked her hair back over her ears. In the dark, we realized the parking gate at the entrance had closed. We couldn't leave now. We owned the place.

I waited weeks for a reminder that I had to put a stop to this. I was the other guy. I didn't even know her middle name and, if I did, wouldn't know what it stood for. This fling would run its course and I would be flung. You're being a sucker, friends said. Nothing good can come from this.

But during the day, meetings or phone calls incessantly preempted discussion. When Cecile and I could, we skittered through it together. I hoped the pheromones wouldn't melt the office router cables.

natm: are you still there
cecilero: y
cecilero: on the newsweek call
natm: what are you doing after work
cecilero: mostly nothing
natm: do you want to meet me at the outside smoking

SAVE FOR FIREFLIES

bench?
cecilero: ok
Pattier: nat get me data on the xnjs results for sony asap

natm: i need just a minute alone with u

Pattier: ??????

natm: Pattie, that was meant for someone else. Results would be fine.

    Summer arrived early. Pattie announced that two clients were cutting P.R. budgets. She used the word "sunsetting." There was no reason to worry. The industry was merely shifting gears, she claimed. For real growth, pruning and weed-pulling was needed. Metaphors continued to be mixed.

natm: maybe you and i could sunset
cecilero: are you trying to hit on me?
natm: how could i say it in french?
cecilero: do not try

natm: adieu soleil
cecilero: maybe we can communicate in small faces :   )
cecilero: @~ ~ **/ ~ ~@
natm: what does that one mean?
cecilero: i made it up. it is something new and enormous

Cecile couldn't sleep at night. I savored my delusions. We were both losing weight. We ate only cheddar popcorn for lunch, sometimes splitting a bag from the snack tray and flopping onto the inflatable furniture in our media room. We'd try not to touch hands while we watched CNNfn, formulating reasons why a show didn't feature our single remaining client's CEO.

Cecile and I might exist in another blip on the digital landscape, one with the usual binary rhythm of one and twos, and we'd be saved. But never on this one, with the looming third party. I'd need to hand in my notice to Pattie.

The PowerPoint slides started to pulsate by 9:30. I took a break to draft a resignation letter and a long e-mail to Cecile, where I got stuck on the last word explaining the bad decision of clamping the rest of her life into a marriage. Just the right word, or *le mot juste*, would allow her to see it. I switched back to the resignation letter instead, which danced merrily out of my fingertips and into the Word document I printed out on company letterhead and left the office with.

On a cold summer night after a colder summer day, I took the highway loops home at 90 miles an hour. I could feel the decomposition of the highways. I went home alone out of the flat, sandy ground of the Silicon Valley. The Oracle headquarters gleamed on my right like a fortress of mirrors with no apparent door or windows. In the dusk, I imagined foundations tipping into sinkholes and lagoons drying up. I saw the airport vanish and wires strung along the highway snap away from the timber of telephone poles. Concrete crumbled under my tires and pink stucco houses blew off the ridge like sand castles. Soon my tin car would fall away by part, until I was gently skidding along the dust of an untouched peninsula. I was four hundred thousand years old, intruding on barren soil and moving with fossils that never had to question their motives or the substance of things they couldn't touch.

natm: this is the last time i'll see you
cecilero: don't like the sound of it
natm: tough
cecilero: yes it is
natm: we'll meet at the hotel?
cecilero: room 219
cecilero: and there is no laughing around here anymore
natm: no most certainly not

We had one night before she would leave for France for a month. For the evening and through to the next sunny morning, this subject never came up. We had no words left for it.

It was a June wedding. Cecile would match the flowers in her bouquet to the flowers in the aisles. I'd entered her life too late into the preparations. Pulling back at this moment might be disastrous for the two of us and our long-term prospects. She had to get married first for us to ever work. It sounded like a justification only when I explained it to perplexed outsiders.

In the office, colleagues offered misty-eyed congratulations the day before she left. "It's like a fairy tale," Pattie stated. I signed my name on the greeting and registry gift card that had been passed around among us as a token of our deeply joyous best wishes.

Some things just weren't possible. The objection to the wedding, where we raced out of the back of the church tossing her white veil onto the congregation aghast, never happened.

I would give up elsewhere. I'd start with the job.

natm: i'm quitting for real this time

Cecilero is offline

It would be the beginning of slow year of excruciating patience realizing, as we both did once she returned to this savage country, that from here and despite ourselves, we would only last.

– – –

In our insect-splattered, duct-taped jalopy, Cecile and I and Julie and Louise crossed the length of highway 101 north.

We passed the Foster City exit, where the window of our old building held a large "Office Space for Rent" sign. The Silicon Valley branch of the agency had shut down all operations a couple years after Cecile and I had both quit. We passed the offices of a few old clients, who had since removed their name from the side of the building leaving only the pegs that once held the sleek letters of their start-up.

Cecile and I were an idea just as ludicrous. I'm sometimes tempted to say I was as surprised as everyone else that we lasted, but I really wasn't. We had fallen for each other with the real sense that, over the proverbial long haul, we might endure. Otherwise, I would never have taken the gamble.

I'd waited for her through two sad, ragged years after her wedding, during which we stole early evenings and infrequent nights wondering why this was happening. Cecile finally reversed the course of her life. She balked at the expected marriage to her old French boyfriend whom, it took her an oceanic emotional change to admit, she no longer knew and no longer loved.

The traffic slowed to its rush hour crawl by SFO airport. We sidled into the car-pool lane that pushed us ahead four or five car lengths until we rolled to a stop again. The vehicles congested into the familiar endless bottleneck.

We were in no hurry. We were experiencing the opposite of road rage. On this inbound trip, the congestion was only prolonging the jolt of recognition we were both absorbing.

"How many times did I drive this road wishing you were coming back with me?" I commented.

"Not as many as I did," Cecile said back, hushed.

The fog hit as soon as we touched down off the highway onto Market Street. We rolled up the windows and pulled on sweatshirts. We came in from summer and entered the refrigerated urban biosphere of San Francisco.

We arrived that night for my brother's second party celebrating his birthday, the one his friends were throwing. This one, by contrast, would be held in an art gallery space with his twenty-something friends and was bound to go all night.

We met Whit on his turf this time. He'd lived in the city for a year now, well after Cecile and I had left. Our girls ballooned into the house he shared with two other roommates. They poked their uncle before settling down for extended petting of the startled housecat. I looked out at his back window toward the view onto Portero and Bernal Hills.

"We can even hang out in the playground around the corner," I told Whit.

"What? There's a playground?" This hadn't shown up on his radar. For Cecile and I, it was the first feature of the neighborhood we'd noticed. We left the city wild and scandalous and returned as boring parental units.

But we were here for a party. We showed up early as Whit's friends set up speakers and a film projected onto the far wall, opposite the beer keg and bottles of tequila. The film would be Fellini's 8 1/2, tonight set to the sounds of electronica music and genres of rock I didn't have the proper names for. Julie and Louise bounced around on the haphazard array of sofas in the otherwise wide-open, high-ceilinged warehouse. As guests trickled in, they took one look at the girls and wondered if they'd come to the wrong place. To find anyone under the age of eighteen at one of their friend's party was an unsettling curiosity.

Julie knew she'd entered an environment typically reserved as adults-only and was proud to be, for once, included. Louise sat on the floor on a throw pillow gazing up at the circus images from the Fellini film. She was riveted like it was an episode of Clifford the Big Red Dog.

<u>Conversation Topics with Various San Francisco Party-Goers</u>
* whether or not kids understood Fellini better than adults
* what my brother was like in college
* whose idea it was to put the images of a penis and breasts in icing on his birthday cake
* who would be warning me when the cake comes out so that my girls don't go grabbing for it
* the meaning behind another friend's art installation which included raw meat being shot out of a cannon
* another guest's timely wedding which she and her partner had celebrated before same-sex marriage was made illegal in California
* the roads we took to get here

* how we should stay for Burning Man in September
* how this whole evening's hedonistic scene would probably suffice

Julie and Louise took it upon themselves to mingle, serving pretzels and chips. Though the volume in the room had grown louder and the kinetic energy that any good party eventually takes on had become palpable, the girls were fading. We reclined Louise in her stroller and stretched Julie out on the couch to see what would happen. Within minutes, they'd both dozed off. They'd officially joined the ranks of the world's most extreme survivalists. They'd managed to fall asleep amidst the wilds of a bass-thumping San Francisco Friday night party.

As dancing broke out and people adjourned for something happening on the second floor the details of which I didn't want to know anything about, Cecile and I scooped up the girls and got a ride back to our camper.

We climbed into the familiar sleeping quarters. The incline we'd parked on, which looked mild from the outside, caused Cecile and I to roll steadily into one another against the back door. But after a day that began at the base of a redwood on the other side of this elongated state, we were too beat to care.

We woke up that morning on the curb of 24th St. in Noe Valley, gravity having snuggled Cecile and me together in the back.

Out of the camper in the clothes we'd slept in, we tried to blend in. Other parents our age talked into cell phone ear pieces while pushing their kids in military-grade strollers. Various window-shopping couples wore outfits indistinguishable from pajamas matched with expensive, spotless sneakers.

We ambled a few blocks to a breakfast spot called Toast Eatery that was new and packed with more of the same crowd trying to show off how rumpled they could look. My clothes/pajamas/camping outfit was either just perfect or horribly embarrassing, I couldn't tell which.

On the Toast Eatery menu, everything was fresh, fair-trade certified, proudly organic and prepared with a stylish twist. It was the first breakfast we'd come across, having by now sampled a range, where the omelets came with chicken apple sausage and the pancakes with macadamia nuts. It was also the first establishment that charged nigh on ten dollars for them. All of it, however, was terrific and you didn't walk out of the place feeling sluggish and exhausted from lard consumption the way you did, for instance, at an IHOP or Denny's.

After showering and doing some laundry at Whit's place, we walked through more of the Saturday morning scene in the neighborhood, coming upon a bustling market, pushing as many political grass-roots causes as locally-grown produce.

"Are you into solar?" a man with a North Face fleece vest over a blue Oxford shirt asked.

"Yes, but we live in France, so…"

"Oh then, you must already be way ahead of us."

I didn't take the time to explain to him the French continued their ongoing love affair with nuclear power and that I'd met more French persons who believed that global warming was an elaborate hoax than Americans.

Instead, I asked for his angle on solar. He had a petition for a project called One Block Off the Grid. It had just begun that summer as a competition among the city's districts to get as many residents as they could to rely on renewable energy sources, namely solar, and exist independent of the city power grid. Noe Valley was ahead of much of the rest of the city, he told me. He already had a long list of names.

"Keep up the good work, Europe might not be as far ahead of you as you think," I told him and walked on. Though I wasn't in the proper political or sociological frame of mind to dive into these or other issues, I lingered with the girls, as Cecile took time to shop, enjoying the display of a people tackling huge problems for themselves and volunteering to be the ones who'd be finding and then implementing a solution. I hadn't been exposed to this positive spirit of knowing there was a better solution in my years abroad.

I wanted to stay to help. But I was nothing but an approving observer. Bouncing around the country, never staying in one location for more than a night or two, gave me this privilege. It had been the case since I'd left the US, I realized. I didn't feel a sense of responsibility to any particular community or nation. While I had emotional investment in the changing U.S. political scene, it no longer directly affected my daily life. At the same time, I hadn't spent enough time in France yet to experience gut-level reactions to what happened within the networks of power in Dijon or the French republic. I had circled the wagons instead, which comes with both being a foreigner and responsible for the mini-community that is your vulnerable family unit. Doubling down on this sensibility on this voyage, our wagon, the Cruiser Royale, and its contents had become the whole of my world.

But life was not lived this way. We'd needed a community to return to, whether our current hometown or not, and whether or not I was yet ready to make a substantial contribution.

We toured the city for the morning and afternoon, like the happy tourists we still were. But the highlight of the day, and what ended up being something to remember the entire trip by, was driving out to the Lands' End Trail, on the northwest horn of the San Francisco Peninsula at the end of Geary Boulevard, past my old apartment.

We ran down the slope from the parking lot at Land's End to the walking path that curved from Ocean Beach. We followed the rugged pines growing on the cliff until we spotted the Bay and the Golden Gate Bridge, stunning and stalwart as it presented the endless sky and sea to the glittering city behind it. The Golden Gate Bridge declared something akin to "Welcome to a place completely out of this world."

From the main paved path at Land's End, a dozen side trails, most of them unofficial, led to the cliff's edge high above the waves that crash into the rocky coastline. When you look closer, you can see the remains of ships wrecked on foggy nights centuries ago. These days, the cargo ships the size of floating islands and marked with Chinese names push straight through, swinging wide of the craggy rocks.

When you squint beyond them, in the hazier distance, the green and gold Marin headlands rise above the shore and roll north.

Louise broke into her gallop along the Land's End trail, trying to keep up with the Pacific wind gusting around the bluff. Julie danced and twirled. Both of them perhaps felt how transfixed and how happy Cecile and I were.

Cecile and I stared at the Marin headlands Cliffside, just to the left of the bridge, toward that patch of high grass where we'd talked well into the morning hours, listening to the currents and the foghorns and feeling our lives tack like lost ships toward one another.

If not for that early replete moment, our attraction may not have flourished and Cecile eventually would have left for France in a miserable relationship, while I would have stayed, periodically visiting the viewpoint by myself, without her or any inkling of the two little girls who now hopped toward the seagulls by the ocean view.

It was enough to give a person an indestructible faith in geography. It was enough to give a person faith, in whatever form it came available.

While this unspoken tribute to hope realized reverberated between Cecile and I, we nearly forgot the present. Standing here now also meant we'd reached the terminus of the continent. This spot was the conclusion of the New World, where the road mile markers and dust clouds stopped and the vast story we'd just been witness to slipped into an underwater continental shelf. The overlook had been named as such for a reason.

SAVE FOR FIREFLIES

We could no longer drive any farther away. We'd found Land's End. From here, we could only take the road back.

SAVE FOR FIREFLIES

NORTH - - -

Louise lifted her eyes toward the window. Her thumb had returned to its snug home inside her mouth, while the four other fingers of the hand held tight to her cuddly plush toy, a pink and yellow rabbit referred to by the French noun, *doudou*. Her free hand played with the floppy, fraying ear. Outside the window, the hills of the Sonoma wine valley sped across her field of vision. Louise would be asleep in five minutes, but she kept this pose of contemplation until her eyelids couldn't hold themselves up any longer.

Julie broke the silence.

"I have a question now. We are going where?" she asked dropping her own thumb and *doudou* for a moment. She piqued Louise's interest too, who tore away from the window.

"We're leaving the city of San Francisco," I responded as accurately as I could.

They both then returned to the unfurling scene outside and rocking motions of the highway, the Golden Gate well behind us. Louise let her brown eyes close on the afternoon sun. We would drive north on 101 until Cloverdale, where we'd exit onto Rt. 128 toward Mendocino and the coast. From there, we'd still only be leaving San Francisco.

It had been a total of five days. On that second one, after catching the sunset from that forever overlook at Land's End, we returned to my old apartment at 12th and Clement St. in the neighborhood sometimes referred to as New Chinatown, a friendlier, less piled-on alternative to the tourist stop of San Francisco's downtown Chinatown. I parked the camper on the strip of greenery lining Park Presidio Boulevard as though I still lived around the corner in the second floor apartment with old friends, as though I'd be meeting them for beers at the Bitter End or the Plough and Stars pubs. Because it felt like home, it felt safe and we would spend the night on the street.

So we would sleep three nights along the street curb. Enough to get a partial glimpse, still a very cushy pantomime, of what it would be like to be a part of the city's burgeoning and uniquely visible homeless population. We didn't actually mean to keep doing this, as we had several friends in the city welcoming us into their homes, but each night the more convenient option was to stay with the accustomed sleeping arrangement.

With one of these friends, we probably shouldn't have resisted the extension of hospitality. We met Erik and his wife, Melissa, and their four-year-old boy. I had an instant, familial affection for their little guy. He toddled around and I saw my friend in him, the same grin and earnest focus in his eyes, proffering a tidier version of his father. Maybe I just missed boys in general, who horsed around, even at age four, in a fundamentally opposite way. Erik seemed just as surprised by my girls.

"Oh, they're squeaky," he noted as Julie and Louise roamed around the playground.

After dinner, Erik and I we went out to a bar to chortle and cry together into our beer about everything we hadn't been able to share in real-time during these intervening years. We talked about our kids, the work he was looking for having just finished grad school studies in architecture, the new De Young Museum design, our wives, our parents, ourselves turning into them and about other travels that lay ahead. Then he posed the question, "So what else have you been thinking about lately?" which meant something larger.

It was the kind of starter question for nearly every conversation in college, that wound through all-encompassing, metaphysical ideas or else deeply sarcastic, immature wisecracks and, whenever possible, both at the same time. After college, Erik had left for the mountains of Sikkim, a province in Northern India, where he'd studied with Tibetan monks and engaged in month-long sessions of Buddhist meditation. I typically waited for him to provide me with answers. He'd assumed that role for me well before he'd ever begun his Eastern voyages to look for his own.

Erik was one of a precious few persons in the world I would turn to if all else in my life had fallen to pieces. I'd always counted on the fact that he'd be there, willing to listen as I explained how it had come to this.

But now what had I been thinking about lately? Purpose and the forest for the trees had become slightly irrelevant topics in these doing years. The answers we've come up with were manifested in the new people in our lives. The only real question I had was what we were doing here as happy, responsible fathers with only an hour or two in five years to reconnect and pose these kinds of questions to one another. If he and I were mild-mannered, inveterate searchers, a characteristic which in college had glued us so immediately to one another, where did we stand now? Had we ourselves fallen to pieces without realizing it? Were we soon unrecognizable to one another? I came up with very little at the time, but promised myself I'd get back to him after I'd thought about his question for the next five thousand miles.

 The next night we had dinner with an old friend and colleague from that now nonexistent Silicon PR agency. Only a passing mention was made of the wild scandal that Cecile and I had kept hushed until long after we'd all quit our jobs there. It turned out coworkers knew something was up. We were able to joke about it now, though I couldn't fully relinquish my paranoia in keeping the story and the affair under wraps. The details were less important by now. We still bonded though over making fun of our old boss.
 This friend had settled down with her husband and young daughter in Asbury Heights, in a three-story house with ceiling-high windows with views onto Golden Gate Park and the Upper Haight district. Their family had an ideal setup where one couldn't be in want of anything else, just as Erik and his family did living close to the top of Bernal Hill in the quiet neighborhood of Bernal Heights.
 All these heights amidst all this ripe opportunity, how could one ever say no to this city? That night, I left the moms

to catch up once the kids were in bed and, for one last spree, I traipsed out into city nightlife while I still could.

I met my brother at the Zam Zam bar on Haight St. where the décor was something resembling a Turkish harem room. He sat me down and ordered drinks for the both of us while the quiet ambiance of the bar on a weekday night soon transformed into the center of town around which all the rest of the clowns, flower children, geeks, blowhards and young, aspiring parents seemed to be revolving. The evening launched off from there, ending many hours later, as these evenings often tend to, at a corner donut shop.

Cecile believes San Francisco holds enough sway over anyone who moves to the town that it significantly alters their world-view within months. This quality had swayed her. But we knew others whose perfectly contented coupling had been upended when one or both parties relocated here. This had happened, for instance, to my brother when he left New York City for San Francisco and he agrees with Cecile's theory. It's the otherworldliness and array of lifestyle possibilities on synchronous display that makes any relationship doubt its stasis.

My take is that the denizens of San Francisco share such an unquenchable thirst for self-actualization that there's little time for taking a committed interest in one single other person. Whether aiming to be the most carbon-footprint-minded person they know or the most healthy in mind and body because of the daily unicycle-riding they do or the most impactful because of the people they're non-profit reaches out to or the most leading-edge because of the paradigm their company's open-sourced operating system is shifting, the devotion to bettering self and world can crowd out any personal relationships.

But with all the steadfast enrichment, a deceptive brand of competitiveness has crept into the San Francisco lifestyle that has steadily exterminated the kooks. The antics of the natives have turned self-conscious and goal-oriented. The atmosphere of the town, if there is one, is anathema to the traditional trajectory of growing up. A Bay Area lifestyle doesn't fit with the conventional journey where one settles down and makes choices in life that sometime require sacrificing oneself and one's individual happiness. Instead, the thinking goes, why would anyone ever bother with a thought or activity that's not personally rewarding?

There's another irony then in this otherwise irony-free zone, one that I never spent much time contemplating when I lived there. San Francisco, as people everywhere else seem to remember first, marks itself as dead center on the fault line between the Pacific and North American tectonic plates.

A report issued by a federal disaster assessment agency in the year 2000 listed the top three most likely catastrophes that lay in America's future. These were 1) a large-scale terrorist attack in New York City 2) a hurricane-induced flood in New Orleans and 3) a devastating earthquake in San Francisco. So if we're keeping a tally that makes two down. Just one to go.

But more seismic for Cecile and me is the personally historic fact that San Francisco will always be a starting block, the launch pad for the rest of our lives together. Considering a return there one day might just be tampering with whatever kooky magic we have left.

So it shouldn't have been surprising that Cecile and I felt directionless after crossing the Golden Gate Bridge once again. Thus, the reason I didn't have an actual answer for Julie about where we were going. Whatever lay ahead on the trip- the sights, the people waiting, my dutiful itinerary - it was hard to ignore that, for the first time, we had more miles behind us.

I took the most reliable course of action, the one we'd always chosen when unsure or undecided: go further.

While we steered through the dry, yellow grass and scrubby trees along the two-lane Route 128 that lead to the coast, Cecile and I talked.

"I miss Dijon," Cecile sighed.

"Really?"

"I miss our apartment, a little. Don't you?" Cecile tagged on a question, double-checking my willingness to return to France.

"Verdict's not in yet," I replied. "I just can't believe Miss Let's-Eat-Asphalt wants to go back to Dijon already."

"I didn't say I want to go back yet. At least, I'm not trying to move us here."

"I haven't been saying that...yet."

"Anyway, the point is you're happier with old friends."

"What makes you say that?"

"You're like a kid again around old friends. You're less serious."

"I'm not serious ever."

"That makes me say whatever. You're always huffing and puffing at every little thing."

Cecile waited for my huffy retort.
"So now you're mad," she confirmed.
"No. You're exaggerating though."
"I don't think so."
"I'm not the one accusing the other of being miserable."
"That's not what I said! Now who's exaggerating?"
"What do you mean?"
"This is exactly what I'm talking about. Then you make me out to be the mean one."
"Ok, settle down for a second."
"I don't like being put in this mean role."
"I don't want to get into this. With such nice scenery too."
"Fine, *bien sur, c'est ma faute*."

Route 128 emerged from the low woodlands and spilled onto the coast. We turned right onto California 1. This mythic road that traced the western edge of the continent was elevated high above the deep blue water of the Pacific. The sun had been gone long enough that the purple glow over the horizon had spread and diffused into the sky. At the Van Damme campground, just south of the town of Mendocino, the state park staffer at the entrance booth had one last site available.

The air just off the beach and inside the forest cover was moist without being humid. Though we hadn't arrived at the redwood forests yet, the woods had taken on that deep green kingdom air that characterized the northern California coast. In the Van Damme campground, the facilities, the telephone poles and the low fence around the trickling stream were constructed from the wood of the surrounding trees. The red timber had been split and chopped into something purposeful, but soon enough, it had gathered layers of moss, lichens and a seeped-in moisture that had turned the wood back into something resembling its original state. Now, the forest was reclaiming the planks. The trees had reanimated their felled cousins.

We made a fire that night with redwood logs purchased in town. I needed only two or three for the evening, as each log burned at least twice as long as the standard pine. The embers glowed like fresh lava for hours and hours, giving me the time I needed that night to decide where we were all headed and what shape the rest of our days, on the road and beyond its now perceptible end, might take.

Up the road from our campsite the next morning, the path to the Point Cabrillo Lighthouse wound through tall dry grass that could have passed for a wheatfield. The looming redwood forests were out of sight. Among the grasses between the highway and the water, we could have been in Kansas if we confined our field of vision only to the foreground. But the illusion dropped off into the blue surf pounding into the cliffside. The wind whipped and roared off the water at us.

We ducked inside the lighthouse. The Point Cabrillo Light Station would, in the following year, celebrate its centennial birthday. It was a shorter and stouter structure than many of the prototype lighthouses of the eastern seaboard, but held an enormous lens and bulb, which could be seen for fifteen miles. The lighthouse was built to support the lumber industry, as boats once docked nearby to pick up the never-ending shipments of axed trees. Those days had, for the most part, passed and now the lighthouse simply staked an elegant claim on this promontory jutting into the sea.

On the lower level, we looked over old photographs and talked briefly with a kind-eyed gentleman who was a guardian of the lighthouse. He was also working the register of the gift shop area that sold wares helping to pay for its upkeep.

I ran through again the thought of what if. What if Cecile and I had parted ways early on and I had chosen a life away from the city, for instance, as a lighthouse keeper? Would this have been a more fulfilling path providing a deeper sense of satisfaction? Would guiding the occasional ship to shore and selling lighthouse sweatshirts be exactly the kind of career move I needed? Without the responsibilities of children and spouse, would I come to appreciate the essence of things through a more deliberate, solitary existence?

My guess is no. In fact, after a week or so in this gorgeous, lonely tower, I would have certainly gone insane with boredom. I would be utterly lost at sea.

Meandering further up the coast, we pulled through Arcata, an otherwise archetypal American rural town and a home to Humboldt State College but with a downtown square, called the Plaza that held a crowd of hangers-on and traveling iconoclasts camped out in the grass with grimy backpacks and juggling sticks like they were waiting for a festival to begin. I got the feeling that in Arcata, if they waited long enough, one would kick up.

This was the town with the first city council in the nation to pass a law nullifying the U.S. Patriot Act, enacted as part of the War on Terror following September 11. Several years later, Arcata also passed a resolution demanding the impeachment of George W. Bush. It's furthermore been said that employment figures are tough to gauge here because of the percentage of Arcatans involved in the cultivation and subsequent big business of cannabis. Just another example of American small-town values.

With the only substances stashed in our vehicle being fever reducer and children's anti-diarrhea formula, we settled in at a coast campground, just north of Arcata, where the shoreline pulled away from the lofty trees.

Clam Beach was the widest stretch of beach I'd ever set foot on, like a cooler Sahara between the land and the sea. The wind blew surface grains over crests, creating ripples so that the whole beach appeared to be moving with its own undertow that paralleled the ocean's. Above the bluster, we heard the sound of the tide. Four or five rows of raging breakers crashed onto the shore. Even if the water wasn't too frigid for swimming, it would have been too rough to stand in. Above us, a front of fog rose in the horizon, which the sun would soon be setting into.

"Let's go put our feet in the water!" I suggested. But the girls froze in place.

At so many stops on our trek I'd told them to be careful. Too many times I'd said watch your step, don't go any further into the woods, don't get too close to that slope or ditch or drop-off, look out for animals, sharp rocks or thorns and, always, don't go too far. There had been one too many moments in the full bloom of Mother Nature where I'd demanded they stay put. Now was a good place to dial down my worry and let go.

"Go ahead and run. You can go as fast and as far as you want," I said. Granted complete freedom, they balked.

Then, I murmured in Louise's ear and pointed to the horizon line before us. "Louise. Ocean."

Louise had never touched saltwater in her life. The thunderous waves were something from a storybook. The expression that spread across her face at the sight of them showed that she realized the word "ocean" meant something even more vast than the blue pages of her board book with the happy whale on it. She recalibrated the size of world again from the top of that dune, one that now had to accommodate something like this.

I scrambled down the dune first. They followed and soon skipped ahead of me, cautiously reassured. They jumped in and out of the holes in the beach formed by the ceaseless gust. Louise toppled over at one point. The wind knocked her entirely on her back. This would usually be a call for crying, but the soft ground made the fall a pleasant surprise. We rolled around together. Some of the sand drifts were big enough for them to hide behind. I took pictures and ran ahead again. We came to the water's edge. We played to see who could get the closest when the tide was out, and then scurried back as a wave tore after us. We turned back toward the shore and made shapes with our shadows elongated into giants over the contours of the sand.

I didn't need to think ahead. I didn't need to play the role of a father either. For the moment, I warned of no danger nor drew any boundaries. Julie and Louise became two people I was lucky to have met.

If I happened to be a guy blessed to find these charming folks out on the beach, it was then with a still greater sense of miracle that we returned to find a woman with blonde-brown hair whistling as she set out the tablecloth and plates on a picnic table for our dinner that night.

"Hey, look who it is!" I said. "Cecile, you've gotta to take a look at the beach."

"So are we done fighting?" I asked from behind the wheel the next morning.

"Fighting!? What are you talking about?"

"The other day, about me being unhappy with you and family life, remember."

"Oh, that wasn't a fight," Cecile shook her head.

"Then we're done with whatever it was."

"What was your point again?"

"That I'd never want to go back to being single and hanging out in bars with my old friends every night."

"What was mine?"

"I don't know. That I'm too serious."

"Sounds like something I would say."

"So if that wasn't a fight, this isn't a resolution."

"Now you have a better point," she conceded.

"Hey, look, here's a nice town, Trinidad. Look at these old houses tucked back into the woods. There's even a harbor. Do you want to stop and take a look?"

"Did you take a wrong turn somewhere?" Cecile said, looking out the back window.

So we moved on. The old trees grew taller and loomed over everything else. The sun peeked through in rays onto the road still less frequently. A herd of elk grazed in a clearing. A log cabin selling totem poles and other things carved from the trees advertised Bigfoot lore. The air grew chillier and, for the first time on the entire journey, we'd switched on the heat in the camper.

I then choose another scenic route, the Newton B. Drury Scenic Parkway, which lead us into the incomparable majesty of the redwoods. The current coastal redwoods standing in Redwood National Forest are slightly younger (a mere 1,000 years old) and leaner and taller than the Sequoias of the Sierra range on the southern side of the state. This species of trees were the dominant vegetation during the age of dinosaurs and once spread throughout North America. But along the northern California coast, thanks to the persistent presence of mist and general lack of seasons, the prehistoric trees still thrive.

The trees also grow closer together in the northern coast, making for fewer gaps in the forest canopy. This creates darker groves that appear to exist in some middle-strata of nature, both subterranean and lofted above the rest of the world, where the constant moisture not only nourishes trees, but ferns with broad, uncoiling fronds at their base and moss draped over the low hanging branches.

Whereas the Sequoia Park trees of the southern half of the state offer mountain bulk and hardiness, the taller coastal trees, growing in these dense numbers with lower tangled limbs and swelling burls had an uncanny ancient life of their own.

Maybe it was just this mist or maybe something Bigfoot had done, but, unlike in other forests, it was almost impossible to ignore the feeling that here we were among a population of living things that had pushed toward the sky long before any other beings on the planet and would remain long after. Was it preposterous to think they might be watching? Within the deep furrows of their bark, was there something sentient there? Had I just been in California too long?

Three state parks are grouped together inside the national Redwood preserve, Prairie Creek, Del Norte and Jebediah Smith, all of which feature extended trails, camping and well-worn paths encircling the mystic trees.

The Jebediah Smith Redwoods, further inland than the others, held a spot called the Grove of Titans. These were some of largest of the coastal redwoods, the superlatives among superlatives. The trees here are given names like Lost Monarch, Stalagmight and the Screaming Titan. Information as to the whereabouts of the Grove of Titans is nearly impossible to come by, as naturalists and other tree enthusiasts work to keep the place secret and safe from adoring hordes. I'd never seen the grove in person, only pictures of determined fanatics posed before the discovered redwoods like happy ants.

We stuck to the main road. We even found ourselves drawn in to the tacky Trees of Mystery tourist stop in Klamath, thanks almost exclusively to the Paul Bunyan and Babe the Blue Ox at the entrance that we couldn't resist letting the girls see. This Paul Bunyan statue also spoke, answered questions and waved hello, all via a piped-in PA system and a lookout booth positioned nearby.

The girls were startled by this sight and wary when the Paul Bunyan statue personally welcomed them. Julie soon tried to offer him a cookie while Louise attempted to wrap her arms around the toe of his black boot. Several visitors started casual conversations with the animatronic lumberjack.

Things Overheard from the Talking Paul Bunyan Statue
* "Welcome to the Trees of Mystery in the beautiful California Redwoods!"
* "I'm over 36 feet tall!"
* "This is Babe the Blue Ox beside me."
* "No, he's not a cow, he's an ox."
* "No, I don't get bored standing here, I get to meet people such as yourself."
* "Actually, I was born in Bangor, Maine in a cradle so big my parents had to rock me to sleep with the ocean waves."
* "Well, do you know how the Grand Canyon actually formed?"
* "Sure, my axe is big enough."
* "Well, I won't talk about that, but my arms are over 15 feet long."
* "Yes, I've always had a beard."

* "No, I don't think anybody's annoying!"
* "Hey, there's someone wearing a hat. Nice hat, sir, please let me personally welcome you to the California Redwoods!"
* "You know, the Yuroks refused to enter the trees because they thought they were sacred."
* "Enjoy, your tour of the Trees of Mystery, the ticket booth is just off to my left."

In lieu of a daring trek down the darker trails of the redwoods, we followed Mr. Bunyan and the trail of the Trees of Mystery. The girls scrambled up the trail like excited forest gnomes.

The trail featured audio stops along the way with red buttons beside a speaker box that when pressed told you what a nurse log is or more about how the Yurok Indians refused to even enter these woods out of spiritual reverence (begging the question of our presence yet again). The trail showcased relief carvings recounting famous American folktales, like the life of Bunyan and Rip Van Winkle, in an amateurish style that made the sculptures and its canned audio accompaniment creepier than they needed to be. Julie and Louise soon realized the audio commentary restarted each time the button was pressed. The sounds of "It was here that…it was here that…it was….it….it…it" resounded through the forest until we steered clear of the buttons altogether.

We ended at the SkyTrail, a gondola lift through the forest. The girls pressed their faces to the glass as we zipped up the incline and above the treetops. We stepped out of the gondola at an altitude well above the forest cover. From this vantage point, I squinted east over to the sea of evergreen. Somewhere among them was the Lost Monarch redwood, still waiting for others to discover its hidden throne, with plenty of time to let the rest of us do all the talking.

- - -

In Dijon, I'd come to love the kitchen. When time allows for planned meals, cooking is, without question, my favorite homemaking responsibility. I've learned to cook French dishes from recipe books, one for rabbit fricasseéd in red wine, another for pork cooked with a tarragon Camembert sauce. Over a cutting board or a saucepan, I devote inordinate amounts of time to each ingredient.

On the road, though, Cecile was the head chef. My close attention to recipes had been left back in Burgundy. We had almost fully remolded into traditional gender roles by now. Surrounded by my native cuisine and usually famished at the end of the day, my tastes tended toward volume and ease of preparation. In America, I had turned into a Viking again, encouraged further by my near daily exposure to open flames. Cecile, meanwhile, had adopted my role as the patient cook. She experimented in our small but efficient camper kitchen with the organic or Asian or Tex Mex food ingredients that weren't as readily available in France. I had become a barbeque master of the sloppy, fire-blasted and blunder-proof cuisine.

There were two meals I'd come to look forward to ending the day with- Hobo Pies and Frito Tacos. Julie and Louise concurred with me. They were messy meals in which any and all ingredients, in any combination, could be thrown together with abandon.

In my method, Hobo Pies are prepared by placing the base – ground beef, shredded chicken or beans - on a long strip of a double layer of tin foil. I sprinkle cheese over it followed by chopped onions, green peppers and tomatoes. I turn up the ends of the tin foil, forming a receptacle complete with makeshift handles, like a foil handbag of food valuables, which is placed over the grill or set it directly on top of hot coals until the meat is browned and the cheese fully melted. Once I remove it and let it cool, I dive into the splendid mess right out of the foil.

Frito Tacos have similar ingredients, usually with the addition of fresh lettuce, salsa and sour cream, and the presentation is still more barbaric. The meat, beans and cheese are cooked and then placed into a snack bag of Fritos or corn chips and topped with the fresh veggies. Like the hobo pies, this is a meal right out of the bag that, once finished, is crumpled into a neat ball once and winged into the trash.

These are the kind of meals that would make my fellow French compatriots faintish. Most hobos in France wouldn't dare dine this way. Because it would offend my French brethren and because eating in this manner is acceptable nowhere else but over a campfire in a place you've never been before and may never be again, the smorgasbord in foil or snack bag becomes haute-cuisine. By the time we cross back over the continental divide, I suspected, I might reach my lifetime fill. And need wider pants.

I polished off a full foil of Hobo Pie and some of the girls' leftovers at the Grassy Flat campground, miles from the Oregon border and still within what was referred to as the Redwood Empire. We camped that night just outside of the large groves, after getting our first no vacancy of the trip from a park ranger at the Jebediah Smith campground.

The trees at Grassy Flat are shrubs compared to the towering redwoods. We'd picked a site that was well-secluded because of the dense Pacific Madrones, twisty trees with red, peeling bark. They grew not all that much taller than our camper, but carried their own sense of gnarled mystery.

That night, I walked in the dark to fill up our jugs and bottles of water. Everyone was asleep by nine and my small flashlight was the only light around me, save one or two campfires in the distance flickering between the crooked branches and shrubby forest understory. The pump hadn't looked far away when we passed it during daylight hours, but in the chilly darkness it felt like an advanced hike.

After over forty nights lingering outside after dark in the woods, on this night I was scared. It was the first time it had struck me that I could be. Here I let my thoughts run. I imagined the warnings of the Yuroks not to go near the tall trees. My thoughts jumped to the California black bear and continued down this slippery slope to recalling briefly the story of the Donner Party or the man responsible for several murders in Yosemite several years ago. I conjured everything I couldn't see, all that stood in the shadows of the trees and just beyond the circle of my flashlight. I summoned the image of whatever might be there when exposed by my trembling beam of light. I jumped at the sound of a creaking tree branch. I found the pump in these twisted, haunted woods and held the handle of my flashlight in my armpit, the beam trained on the faucet as I filled our canisters.

I scampered like a frightened squirrel back to the site. I leapt inside the camper, convinced something was at my back, inches from grabbing the collar of my shirt. I locked all doors. I made sure the keys were in the ignition, as we'd made a habit of doing, in case a mugger, a maniac, a zombie, a Sasquatch came clawing at our door.

After a few minutes, I breathed a sigh of relief and straightened my posture back into the father and husband whose job it was to reassure everyone else that there was nothing to be afraid of.

I-199 pulled northeast, away from the coast and the mighty redwoods, toward central Oregon and the heart of the Cascades. This range stretches from Mount Lassen at its southernmost point in California up to Lytton Mountain in British Columbia.

I'd heard the Pacific Northwest sometimes referred to as Cascadia. An independence movement has developed. People in the region who feel Washington D.C. doesn't represent their interests have decided to lobby for the Republic of Cascadia, a sovereign nation.

The landscape alone seemed almost too beautiful and untouched to be lumped in with the rest of the continent. We'd been through pretty areas of the country, but few like Oregon which managed to feel contentedly inhabited while remaining pristine and unplagued by some of America's entrenched problems of suburban sprawl, over-commercialization and eye, noise, and air pollution. Should this area ever decide to secede and Cascadia declare its independence, I might hesitate in siding with the remainder of the hapless United States.

The first major town we came to was the friendly, bustling Grant's Pass, which confirmed the good life for us. The town was at a happy crossroads between the highway North to Portland, the exit East toward Crater Lake and the route south to the redwoods. Fringed on all sides by green mountain ridges, Grant's Pass had chain establishments, some traffic and a Wal-Mart but none of it seemed to encroach on the conscientiousness of the people and the fact that, whatever they did, the natural environment was chief among concerns.

From Grant's Pass, we had a short, spectacular drive into the crown jewel of the Cascades, Crater Lake National Park. We could take it slow as we had the rest of the day to reach the Mazama campground inside the park. A guidebook claimed that it rarely filled up even during the high tourist season.

Along the road that steadily climbed toward Crater Lake through the Siskiyou National Forest, we stopped to use the facilities; in our case the unpeopled woods all around us. We got back in the camper and continued moving up in elevation, as the air grew thinner and the coniferous wilderness spread. The forest growth here was organized, compared to the shadowy, overgrown Redwoods or rugged Sierras or the deciduous stick-tangle of the East

Coast forests of my childhood. Douglas firs, all the same size and shape, stood at attention in neat columns, like they'd been planted there, though they'd all grown naturally along this range. We caught the Rogue River through the trees on our left, with pure, white rapids and pumice rock banks. At the village of Union Creek, an older man in a denim shirt sat smoking a pipe on the porch under the "Ice" sign at the rustic country store.

Twenty miles after our bathroom stop I heard these words- "Have you seen Louise's doudou?" Cecile was asking about her plush toy, an item as essential for Louise as one of her limbs, but one that was, rather inconveniently, not attached.

"Doudou!" Louise called out panicked. Cecile rummaged through the closet and peeked under all the seats. *Le doudou* was nowhere to be found.

"I think he was dropped when we got out to pee," Cecile surmised.

"Keep looking," I said.

"Wait, stop the car for a minute."

A group search throughout the camper still left us empty-handed. Louise, by now, had launched into a full-bore alarm and was ululating the name "doudou" to the sky like a tragedy of greater magnitude had never befallen another human being. So we turned around and headed back down the same portion of Rte. 62 we'd come from, all the way back to the pullout where we'd done our business behind the trees.

We hadn't yet lost any items of importance on this trip. It was another distinct advantage of a mobile home; stuff wasn't left behind because it rarely left the roving abode in the first place. But now doudou, this helpless, fraying plush rabbit that carried the faint smell of my younger daughter, probably lay stranded somewhere on the bed of prickly cones and needles.

We passed the Rogue River rapids again where anglers now cast their fishing lines into the river. The man at the Union Creek country store tapped out the remnants of his pipe over a log fence. We finally arrived back at our previous stop and searched the ground, where we'd parked the camper and where we'd walked into in the woods. Cecile looked over at me and we threw up our hands outside of the camper. No doudou.

"Hey Louise, I have this very soft, very nice donkey that grandma got for you at a gift shop in Arizona," I said, switching to plan B, "he's really nice and he's great for cuddling. You could give him a name."

Louise took the donkey in her hands with a frown the size of her whole face. Julie, meanwhile, watched the whole scene clutching tightly to her own doudou, a still more ragged plush toy in the shape of the moon, as she imagined the unimaginable and felt so glad that this was happening to her sister.

"No, no et non!" Louise picked up the trial donkey and chucked it to the floor. The tears were merciless.

"Nice try," Cecile muttered. "Okay, let's drive, because soon it will be time for dinner. I'll keep looking around. *Ne pleur pas, Louise, on va lui trouvé.*"

"Maybe this isn't a good time to mention the low fuel light just went on," I mentioned anyway getting back behind the wheel. I turned on new music in hopes of postponing or, otherwise, drowning out Louise's moans.

We crossed the same segment of road again. I misread the words on a sign for the Siskiyou National Forest this time as the *Sisyphus* National Forest. We zoomed by the country store, where the man with the pipe now stood talking to visitors in the parking lot. He looked at us as we passed, possibly with a sudden sense of déjà vu. We marched on to arrive by late afternoon to the entrance booth of Crater Lake National Park, where we received the Park Service brochures and the summer issue of the Crater Lake newspaper, as was standard in all the national parks. We continued to ascend toward the superstar lake. The forest opened up into wide sections of alpine grassland.

"Look, the map says there's a station in the park. Good thing, because we're churning through gas going uphill like this," I announced.

"*Ca y'est!* Found him!" Cecile called out. She had scoured the entire cabin and retrieved doudou. It had somehow gotten wedged between the back of Louise's car seat and the chair, only inches from her head. Louise threw her arms around the little rabbit and resumed intense thumb-sucking with doudou pressed to her cheek.

"Thank god. Now, we just need gasoline and a place to stay for the night," I concluded optimistic. We showed up to the Mazama village, only a few miles from the lake, where the ranger had news for us.

"Campground's full folks. Gave up the last site a couple hours ago."

"We just missed it then. If my daughter hadn't lost her doudou ..."

"Excuse me?" the ranger said. I'd forgotten how the word doudou, pronounced do-do, sounded in English.

"My daughter lost a toy. But that's...can you tell me where the gas station is?"

"Sure, it's just behind you."

"Great, we're running on fumes I think." I looked over my shoulder at two isolated gas pumps.

"But it's closed."

"What?"

"Yep, we had a fire yesterday. The tanks got emptied. Won't be any fuel available until Monday."

Cecile and I had a duel sinking sensation. How could this have happened? We could either remain in this area for a full two days, hoping for a suitable and inconspicuous spot somewhere in the parking lot near this gas station, or we could go back the way we came, to the station we passed almost an hour ago where I should have filled up.

"Back the way we came," I asked turning to Cecile. She nodded, stunned by the prospect of having to all remain in the car, covering the same ground a third time.

So we performed a U-turn around the Mazama village station and threw the camper in neutral. Gradually, we picked up speed going back down the mountain. We waved once more to the village of Union Creek, with the now unoccupied porch of the country store.

The needle pointed past the letter E on the gas gauge. The girls regarded their car seats as diabolical devices of medieval torture. We reached the bottom of the slight grade and had to shift back into drive.

"There it is, I see it," Cecile breathed. An old-fashioned one-pump stand connected to a mini-mart came up on the right. I pulled the camper in and popped open the gas cap. A woman who'd been standing by the closed entrance approached.

"Sorry, we closed at six," she informed us. Even Julie and Louise understood and gasped in distress. "Just seven miles down the road. They're closing soon too though, better hurry."

So we raced for one last leg, against depleted fuel reserves, against time and distance, still coasting in neutral to get there. On this final push, Julie and Louise had observed the level of high-alert that Cecile and I were now on and whispered quietly to one another.

And we did make it. At the sight of the final gas station, we all whooped and waved our arms around like we'd just finished a triathlon.

As the attendant, a woman in overalls and a red bandana, filled us up, I realized the alarm wasn't quite so necessary. There could be much worse fates than an empty tank of gas.

We ended this day in a miracle masquerading as campground. We returned to Union Creek and the now familiar "Ice" sign. The nearby Farewell Bend campground was well hidden between the road and the river. And they had one site left.

The Farewell Bend sites backed right up into the heavenly Rogue River. At twilight the clear water turned turquoise, a shade brighter than the forest and glossier as it swerved around the trunks of the firs. Above us, the treetops were silhouetted in pale bluish-green evening light. My second wind had kicked in somewhere during the fourth doubling back on the road and I couldn't turn it off. After the girls were treated to hot dogs and s'mores and tucked them into bed, I opened a bottle of wine. Cecile and I toasted with plastic cups to the minor miracle of the road that carried us.

- - -

Crater Lake is Mount Mazama collapsed. Over 8,000 years ago the volcano erupted, creating one of the deepest lakes in the western hemisphere.

We arrived the next day, taking our own sorely beaten path toward the park's ranger booth. At the vortex of the mountain forest, a lake waited as hypnotizingly blue as the warmest coves of the Mediterranean. We stood at an overlook high above the water and the mini-peak of Wizard Island rising from the lake's center. Nothing about Crater Lake seemed out of place. It looked like a product of nature's meticulous harmony, despite that it existed because of a violent explosion and subsequent ruin.

The air from this altitude over the lake was frigid again. If the water of the Rogue River that I splashed into that morning was any indication, the lake temperature was close to arctic. Snow drifts that remained year-round dotted the slopes around the lake.

We wanted to drink in more of the view from another angle. We also wanted to start a snowball fight in July. The full circle drive around the lake, according to the guidebook, took over four hours to complete. We aimed to do a quarter of that and started by pulling off into one of the scenic overlooks. At one stop, we saw that a turnoff half a mile up the road offered better views. Cecile had already begun to take Louise out of her car seat. But we'd only be moving for a few more seconds. There was no point in buckling her back in. "It's just in front of us," I said. "Two seconds." Louise's legs dangled loosely.

"Oh, a deer!" Cecile called out. Rounding the bend, a full grown mule deer appeared, grazing along the shoulder of the road with his nose in the grass. I didn't have time to slow down. I assumed the animal would dash away from the pavement. Instead, as they tend to do, the startled deer sprung in front of us. I got a glimpse of wide eyes by the left of our grill. I swerved and then rammed my foot into the brake pedal, lurching the camper and its contents forward.

We broad-sided the animal. I heard a nauseating thud.

At that same foul moment, we heard a smack from behind us inside the camper. Then Louise shrieking. She had been thrown from her seat. Cecile leapt to the floor between the two bucket seats to pick her up where she lay face down. In a torrent of panic, I steered into the turnoff and switched off the engine.

I looked down to Louise, her face now buried in Cecile's arms. When she turned her face to me I was able to gather she had no cuts, bruises or scrapes. She cried in mighty heaves and held up her hands, the throbbing appendages that had evidently broken her fall. Hurting a deer carried an ironic sting that was there to remind me that I'd also hurt the youngest member of our family. Cecile stepped out of the camper with Louise in her arms. I lifted Julie, spooked silent, out of her seat. When I put her feet down onto the paved scenic turnoff, I noticed my own hands trembling. I scanned the road. The deer was nowhere in sight.

"What happened?" Julie asked.

"We ran into a deer. But he went back into the forest. Let's hope he's going to be all right."

Julie nodded, as serene as her parents were frantic. I walked over to Louise, who had already stopped crying and was staring down at the lake as she sucked her thumb and buried her head in Cecile's neck. Cecile and I let out two separate but equally, unsettled sighs.

As in New Mexico, the calamity came in double-shot. First wasps and wind-damage. Then deer and unbuckled seatbelts. Though this second one had none of the loony mishap of the first. This one was awful. And almost exclusively my fault. Or so it felt.

At this extraordinary sight in the Cascades I stood asking myself just where did we get off forcing our kids into a trip like this, compromising their safety and, in the process, wounding whatever unassuming creature we came across as we invaded their domain. Was this worth it? Is this what you inevitably deserve tempting fate and nature like this? Can you not be so clueless half the time and pay attention, for God's sake?

Louise would be okay and the deer had walked away. But it did little for our guilt. What were we thinking, I kept asking myself.

Danger keeps a close proximity. In Dijon, when I take my girls out to the post office, for instance, we walk a distance of maybe four-hundred yards from our third-floor apartment door to the line at Dijon's central La Poste. There are multiple hazards at each step. First, Julie, Louise and I must make it down the stairs, three flights of a steep, spiral wooden staircase, without a trip or loss of footing from those two, who are either going too fast or acting too goofy, that would send them crashing to the bottom. Outside, as we come upon the central square of the city, Place Darcy, we must typically swing wide of one of the unfed, irritable pit bulls who belong to the young people dressed in black who live day and night in the square. We then must traverse the first crosswalk, taking care that Julie, who no longer holds my hand, stops at the curb and that Louise, who still does, doesn't slip out of my grasp and into the street crowded with city buses, delivery trucks and zippy Vespas. Then, there's the person holding the lit cigarette at Louise's eye level that could singe her face. There's the discarded piece of pastry on the ground that pigeons have been pecking at which one of the girls might get the idea to retrieve and finish, ingesting a host of new and violent germs. Once to the building, the heavy glass doors of the post office always come close to shutting on the girl's hands. Afterward, provided they haven't picked up other germs by touching things at this public space, they run around the outside corner of the post office to hide, where a kidnapper could be waiting just out of my sight.

It could be paranoia or helicopter parenting, but the mundane, quiet daily routine is teeming with disaster, illness and injury. Whether driving narrow roads around a blown volcano or strolling just steps from our home, risk is built-in to childhood. It is perhaps for this reason that children are gifted with the ability to be altogether blind to it.

It was a miracle we'd made it to Oregon. It was a miracle we'd made it to Julie at age four and Louise at age two. It was a miracle we ever got safely down the block to send a single piece of mail.

For lunch, we sat on the lip of the crater. We were all in one piece. We ate sandwiches and cherry tomatoes from bowls overlooking the view and tried to be thankful for an environment all around us whose beauty encouraged us to shake off misfortune and keep going. The snowdrifts, the azure lake and the cloudless sky held us to our end of the journey's bargain.

We would follow the default course of action; keep going. We let the road renew our promise of a forward march. We opted for another long haul that day, all the way to Portland, six hours from Crater Lake. Somewhere around Eugene, we tossed thoughts of a wounded deer and a bump on Louise's head along the side of the road. By Salem, we rediscovered our ability to make-believe once more that the world was a harmless, gentle place.

- - -

In what would be the farthest reach of our trip, to the west and to the north, we found Portland.

Unlike San Francisco, Portland has retained its kook quotient, without feeling the need to advertise it. Despite its progressive politics and bumper stickers that refer to the People's Republic of Portland, it's a city that hasn't yet been polished to a squeaky, modern shine so that the founding population of loggers and longshoremen don't feel like a wholly different past. Where San Francisco has gone through multiple iterations since the gold rush of the mid-1800s that transformed the outpost into a major cultural mecca, Portland seems to have grown more naturally. It has become a sensible, family-friendly place to tend an heirloom vegetable garden, commute to work by bike and generally go about your days making a small difference while caring very little about what other people think of you.

In the Nob Hill district on the northern end of the city, the streetlamps and candles of outdoor cafes were lit. We found a Holiday Inn Express that we couldn't refuse. We dropped off our bags and then walked back down the street, sitting down in a sushi restaurant where the dishes could be immediately lifted from little boats and hauled directly into our mouths. We were all famished. Julie even tried the mackerel.

The next day, Portland presented an extended rhapsody on things western culture does right. The nicest clothing stores sold second-hand threads. The toy stores stocked items on their shelves that treated kids like curious

SAVE FOR FIREFLIES

human beings, and not slaves to instant gratification. The clerk showed us a dollhouse for mouse figurines; approaching the matter with the seriousness that playtime was for kids. The mass transit system was predictably green-conscious, well-organized and had stops at every other block. I also learned that Portland had made a concerted effort to build streets without blocking views onto the distant snowcapped Mount Hood to the east. Like Grant's Pass, the environment here never felt intruded upon, but rather worked around with something as close to grace as urban planning is capable of achieving.

Portland also weaves kids into every activity possible. There are bars like the Laurelwood Brewery with a playroom so that parents can have cocktails while keeping an eye on their tykes. There is a large children's science museum, a swath of 5,000 acres of forested park within the city limits called Forest Park (the largest of its kind in any U.S. city), and dozens of smaller downtown parks with fountains designed around the understanding that, in the summer, kids will want to splash in them. All of this in a manageable city made up mainly of residential side streets. At the same time, Portland is large enough to have an NBA franchise and two separate French-American schools. I had by now painted a full picture of what our life here could be. The only thing missing that I could see was fireflies. My beloved insects never ventured as far as the west coast.

In Portland, I had no itch to keep moving. It might have been a residual effect in the air after Lewis and Clark called this the end of their famous trail that gives the state its name. Like them, I needed to go no further. Our trip had then made two mid-point pivots, at our cliffside spot near the Golden Gate Bridge and then in the streets of Portland that I hoped to get back to as soon as possible.

- - -

I returned to the Simone de Beauvoir travelogue. She observes: "Despite its sprawling cities, its factories, its mechanical civilization, America remains one of the most unspoiled in the world. Man with all his works is a new and sporadic phenomenon here, whose laborious efforts merely scratch the surface of the earth's crust."

She wrote those words over sixty years ago. The average American citizen today might deny it (and I've tested this quote on many who dismissed it as outdated or desperately rosy), but more than half-way around a full loop of the country we found over and over that her insight holds true.

Americans have not yet paved everything into a parking lot or crammed a Starbucks into every available open space. We have exacted painful losses on the natural environment within our borders, but when we peel off the main road, we can enter, if we choose, a dominion beyond our control. There are still open meadows, craggy mountains, dense forests, clear lakes and vast shorelines that overwhelm us. Wandering off into the woods or the hills remains a possibility in nearly every state in the country. This is thanks, in no small part, to people who long ago ventured into these unspoiled spaces and decided to work the rest of their lives to keep them that way.

In the Northeast, locating the wilderness might take more deliberate aim. In Oregon however, it takes only a right turn. Whole corners of the state haven't changed in centuries. Whole patches of Oregon are almost as large as New England itself and devoid of humanity's mark, while neither barren nor inhospitable like the deserts to the south. Instead the land is richly fertile and painted in an emerald green.

After leaving Portland, we hurtled across I-84 East following the Columbia River. I remembered once, prior to this trip, meeting a trucker sipping on a late night coffee at a rest stop. He told me he was from Wisconsin, which he described as "the second most beautiful state in the country." "What's the first?" I asked in turn. Before he downed the last drops of his coffee and wished me safe travels, he replied "Oregon."

We stopped for the night at a campground after the bend in I-84 where the Columbia River Highway became the Old Oregon Trail Highway. There, the sun set over land that was still just being born.

We ate dinner looking out onto a vast grassland plateau. As we finished a black Labrador came sniffing at the girls' ears and licking their faces. The three of them became instant long-lost friends.

"Enjoy it, it goes by fast," I heard a man's voice say.

I turned to look up at an older man in shorts and sandals. He stepped out of the adjacent RV with his wife. His hand already extended and ready to shake mine as he still walked toward me, reminding me instantly of my grandfather and engendering an immediate trust in me. He and his wife were the kind of active seniors we'd encountered everywhere on the road. We learned they were retired living in Spokane, Washington and were currently on a summer road trip to visit their daughter in the Bay Area.

We talked until dark with them, sharing stories of the places to see in the West and hearing tales of the stint he did with the Army in France, "way back in the day."

We all turned in early. Like in New Mexico, I felt safer within the proximity of these grinning seniors. At that particular moment, I had no greater wish for my autumn years than for Cecile and I to stay on the road forever, and stop on occasion to visit our grown-up daughters in San Francisco.

The next morning 84 East took us out of the state. We left Oregon much too quickly. We entered Idaho. The mood dampened further.

<u>My Comprehensive Knowledge of the state of Idaho</u>
* it is by most estimates the most conservative state in the country
* the Ruby Ridge homesteader shoot-out of 1992 didn't end well
* the hilarious 2004 film Napoleon Dynamite about extremely awkward people was set here
* the state's most famous politician was Senator Larry Craig who had a "wide stance" beside men in airport bathrooms
* Ernest Hemingway killed himself here
* the Mormon population rivaled that of Utah
* something about potatoes

At the Idaho border, an official state sign proudly announced that the Idaho welcome center was closed. We continued on in search of a rest area with a picnic table. None materialized. So we pulled over beside a dusty field where a farmer turned his loud tractor in circles over dry wheat crops. We ate lunch there in our folding chairs.

We carried on through Boise, where an extra lane opened up briefly but disappeared after the capital city limits. The state was too wide to cross in one day; we'd need to spend a night in Idaho first. In one of our guides, we noticed a KOA in a town called Mountain Home. It sounded promising.

But as we exited the highway into Mountain Home we soon realized there were two things wrong with the name. The flat landscape provided views onto mountains that seemed to have drifted off to the next county. And the forgotten community of dilapidated ranch houses felt neither homey, nor rugged or rustic. A few busted signs invited travelers to visit the area golf course somewhere also well out of sight. It might have been the most desolate location we'd yet stopped in. But we were too road-weary to push on any further.

The KOA mirrored the nothingness of the rest of the town. The older man behind the desk allowed as few words as possible when checking us in, grumbling at the system computer and letting the telephone ring unanswered. He pointed us to our campsite on the map and sighed when I asked for further information about children's activities.

"We got Indian teepees and a swing," he replied as though it was impossible to imagine wanting anything more.

Saving the excitement of the teepees for later, I took the girls to the rickety, paint-chipped swingset with its view onto a row of permanent trailer homes. We took stock again of what we'd just done and where we'd be going. We spent the evening doing laundry, cleaning out the camper and trying to teach Louise UNO. Later, we were surprised by a working wifi connection. We emailed pictures from scenic places taken elsewhere.

The dull spot made me impatient to jump ahead back east. I had a flash of panic that, with only a few weeks remaining, we wouldn't be able to make it back in time. We had to recross that expanse we'd just conquered. Cecile, on the other hand, wasn't thinking about time, but just home. Mountain Home made her think fondly again, she said, of our cozy apartment that had been quiet all summer.

Things We Were Both Starting to Miss About France
* fresh bread
* variety in cheese and yogurt
* chocolate (the kind that makes Hershey's taste like soft crayon)
* public squares at the centers of town
* restaurants and stores that weren't air-conditioned like meat lockers
* red wine whose taste lingers in your mouth after you've swallowed it
* people who care about how they are dressed when they leave their house no matter how routine the activity

* better maintained public roads and highways with clean, fully-appointed rest stops
* a community where people recognized us

I thought about the past year, beginning really in Fall 2007, that I'd focused so fervently on this summer's road trip. Now I'd started to dream once more of France. The deeper concern was that exposure to another country had instilled a chronic longing for wherever I was not. I'd need to break the habit of looking at the neighbors' greener grass. There was no need to recreate France just yet. I had more terrain to cross and people to reconnect with.

"Are you ready to be done with the trip?" I asked Cecile.

"At this moment, yes."

"We still haven't checked out the teepees," I pointed out, indicating the campsite's major attraction.

"I took the girls while you were checking in."

"Dang. Then I guess we just have to wait until New York before there's anything fun to do again."

Cecile laughed. "We need to start dinner. The girls are tired."

"You think we might have traveled too far?"

"What do you mean?"

"Maybe we've done too much driving, too much racing around from place to place. Maybe it's wearing on the girls."

"No, no."

"Right. So we can keep going?"

"What is our plan for tomorrow?" she changed the subject, moving down the road in her head.

"Yellowstone." I replied.

"And you say too far," she said, as though 'too far' were the two most absurd words to have ever echoed over the high peaks and valleys of family life.

- - -

Things Found In My Cargo Shorts Pockets After Six Weeks on the Road
* wallet and car keys
* a barrette with Cinderella's face outlined in a heart
* two March of Dimes peppermint candies
* a Swiss army knife
* cocktail napkins to the Zam Zam bar on Haight St. in San Francisco
* two Dora the Explorer band-aids
* a leaflet about what to do during a bear attack
* a pinecone Louise had asked me to hold onto
* a dime
* a penny pressed into a flat oval and stamped with the words "I Love You Crater Lake, Oregon"
* a postcard addressed to my friend Erik with a picture of fly-fisherman standing in an Idaho river holding a rainbow trout above the words "It's a Keeper!"

Things We Were Starting to Miss About a Stationary House
* being in separate rooms from one another on occasion
* not having a total dependence on unleaded gasoline
* our own shower and toilet

* our spots on the couch while I wrote/surfed the Internet and Cecile watched late night television
* a bed that was always level
* a dishwasher
* not basing the necessity of a load of laundry on how many quarters we had
* being able to walk around our home in pajamas or underwear
* being able to walk around our home
* not having to put away all our things before bed
* waking up in the morning knowing where we'd be that night

    The next day provided more fodder for the question "What happens in Idaho?" I knew we weren't giving the state a fair chance. It was often said that Hemingway's home in Ketchum held a beauty for him that actually kept his outlook positive. Likewise, the Sawtooth National Forest and the Bitteroot Mountains to the north were evidently breathtaking. I also wasn't much of a fisherman, which, as the postcard indicated, seemed to be the official state pastime. We met other people in Idaho, like the crotchety host at the KOA desk, and, the next day at a restaurant in Pocatello, waitresses who looked bored into a kind of zombie state (though admittedly no worse than the servers in, say, York, PA).
    Idaho held then one surprise for me. I read that the state consistently ranks number two on population list of fastest growing in our union, right behind Nevada. What

we'd just driven through represented rampant, explosive growth. I realized I needed to start paying closer attention.

The mountains and deep forests reintroduced themselves after Rexburg. We soon crossed the Targhee Pass, the Montana border and the continental divide all in one easy mile.

We waited a day to enter Yellowstone. We'd stay at a campground in the outskirts of West Yellowstone. Here, as in places before, Europe was well represented. Julie and Louise found a brother and sister at the camp playground speaking French. Julie inadvertently said "Bonjour" and they all four froze not sure how people they didn't know in this rough-and-tumble place they'd just shown up in were speaking their language. After the pause, the children all proceeded as though they were together at a *cours de recreation* of their own making.

"So tomorrow, we shouldn't plan on finding a campground inside the park, because I haven't booked anything in advance. But we can sleep somewhere on the other side. Maybe in Cody. They'll be a ton of tourists."

"Oh I think we'll be fine," Cecile insisted.

Like clockwork, that morning saw us in line among the four lanes of clogged traffic in front of the Yellowstone's west entrance booths. In guides and in personal feedback I viewed on travel websites, legend had it that campgrounds inside the parks fill up a year in advance. I'd nearly skipped Yellowstone, the reigning king of national parks, for this reason.

But coming in from the west into meadows sweeping toward lodgepole pine forests with shallow clear streams running through them, I saw what an error that would have been. There is a reason this park is so frequented and why this land received the first designation of federal protection by act of Congress a decade after the Civil War. Yellowstone was the progenitor of all these set aside spaces we'd been privilege to.

The long-awaited buffalo sighting (bison please) came within minutes, almost as though on cue. Vehicles had pulled along the side of the road indicating the impromptu attraction. We stepped out of the camper in clear view of the massive animal by a streambed. Julie and I approached, getting within 40 yards, then pushing that sternly recommended distance. From within the coarse fur at his shoulders and head, the animal's eyes glanced at the onlookers whispering and pressing digital cameras from the periphery of his charging range.

Julie wanted to get closer, because as she explained he "looked nice." I grabbed her shoulders as we stood watching to prevent any darting forward. The bison decided upon ambling back over the ridge and out of sight. The people, in turn, filed back up the opposite hill and into their cars.

We pressed on, passing holes in the ground billowing steam. The verdant splendor made it easy to forget that Yellowstone is a volcano. More precisely, Yellowstone is a giant volcanic basin that over geologic time has experienced a series of land-restructuring eruptions. In spots all throughout the park, the ground emits steam or boiling mud, on a barely detectable scale or in reliable, sky-high geysers like the park's prime attraction, Old Faithful.

We got our first up close look at this activity in the Norris Geyser. There, an individual pool called the Emerald basin had a deep green floor and orange-tinged shores more vivid than a fresh oil painting. Always requesting the hands-on experience, the girls expressed their desire to put on their swimsuits and splash around.

"Just my feet, peut-être Daddy," Julie requested.

"I know it's pretty, but do you see the steam there? That water is as hot as fire." The girls' eyes peeled wide and they stared down anew at the emerald pool. Louise grasped at my shirt like the water might try to pull her in. This triggered a series of questions about volcanoes, lava and the center of the earth that was constantly becoming a more hazardous place than they'd imagined.

The crowds, it turned out, circumscribed themselves to a handful of identifiable points of interest, leaving the bulk of the Yellowstone wonderland to a happy minority. That afternoon the parking lot at the Mammoth Hot Springs terraces was full, but the campground at Indian Creek had free space aplenty and few cars on its access road.

Beyond our campsite, we hiked part of a trail along the creek that curved and disappeared behind a curtain of pines, no presence of humans as far as the eye could see.

The next morning, I awoke early. I started the engine, hoping the gentle coast and shimmy of the camper would keep everyone else asleep in back bed and over my head. For twenty minutes or so, I drove feeling like a lucky steward of daybreak assigned to the park.

With light yet to burst over the distant ridge, white fog hung in the forest we were emerging from, like ghosts had passed out only an hour ago and half-dissolved among the pines. Whatever else had happened, the wilds had taken over during the night all around us.

Again, as they had when I'd started the day the same way in Bryce, Julie and Louise woke up giddy and jostling from wall-to-wall. On the southern loop of the park, we stopped along the road after I spotted a family of bull elk slipping through the trees. The largest one, the adult male with antlers like two sturdy trees and full, dark brown fur at his throat, stood closest to the road. The female and the younger elk grazed behind him emerging with the mist of the forest. In all their royalty, they glanced sideways in our direction.

The biologist E.O. Wilson believed that it is our capacity for appreciating other species that principally separates humans from animals. It is our habit as humans to stop and get out of the car when we see a bison grazing in the meadow. Or follow the flight path of an eagle spreading its wings and gliding over a valley. Or see some kind of mirror when a family of elk stand just up the hill from a family who's just stepped out, half awake, of a white rolling metal contraption they call their dwelling. But it's only the humans that recognize themselves and the elk as two sets, and draw a connection.

We humans then have the natural habit of anthropomorphizing animals, whether it's trying to guess what they're "thinking" or ascribing emotions. It is the logical extension of this kind of appreciation. For children, the tendency toward viewing animals in our image is taught early on, by smiling animal cartoon characters who wear our clothes, walk upright and sing songs, making the sight of the real thing a relearning process for kids who expect the ducks in the pond (or the wolves in the meadow) to be their cuddly pals. At the same time, we conversely, remove any trace of a previous existence as animal once we've turned them into meat. The pig is either Wilbur from Charlotte's Web or part of a sandwich between the mayo and the cheese.

In the western half of the U.S., in the rugged patches of the country, animals are still living on their terms and one gets the sense the residents of these open western states don't as easily forget the power that wild animals hold.

As our eyes adjusted to the morning sun, we gazed at the family of elk from the roadside. Soon, they pranced off to further pastures at their own speed deeper into the national park they called home.

"Are we going to the volcano today?" Julie asked.

"Yes, but it's not a volcano, they call it a geyser."

We pulled safely into the lodge parking lot like reentering a metropolis, though we'd been, and were still, within the park all this time. Once we had pressed coffee, juice and airtight-sealed Cheerios, we stepped out to walk among the throngs of those who also hoped they'd timed their visit nicely to Old Faithful. Dry-erase boards tacked up around the area displayed the next eruption time. We still had thirty-seven minutes.

We took a seat on the semi-circle of benches, like we were waiting for a performance to start. The geyser for now was still in the dressing room. Every few minutes, hot water spurted from the cordoned off hole in the ground, causing oo's and aah's to rise from the near standing-room only audience. The water dropped back to a steaming trickle and the ring of cameras fell back into laps. False alarm.

The geyser teased the audience a few more times with what was referred to as preplay before the eruption (as opposed to "foreplay" before the "emission"). Soon people began to complain openly, as though they'd paid good money and nature better deliver, or else.

Then, patience nearly tried, Old Faithful roared toward the clouds, a blast four stories high, misting our faces. It rendered moot most of the anticipation, making just about everyone a little bit frightened as the realization struck that under the soil we'd been waiting on, dubbed America at the moment, all this activity had been boiling over and there was little any of us could ever do to control it. Old Faithful just happened to gargle and explode to a pattern, whereas most beneath the surface it did not. A supposedly dormant geologic feature might see fit to overturn the inn, visitors' center and paved roads back to civilization at any moment. We were here about a volcano, after all.

The eruption lasted for several minutes before Old Faithful settled once more into tranquil steam. Some clapped at the conclusion. I saw a ranger wiping away the nearest eruption time on a dry-erase board and felt-tipping out a new one. The faithful explosion times were calculated based on the duration of the gushing we'd just seen. That Old

Faithful not only went off, but also stopped going off on relative cue provided reassurance. The last widespread volcanic upheaval happened in this park 640,000 years ago. Things were all under control. We could place our faith in nature. Thanks to this stalwart friend of ours, we could rest easy knowing the geothermal park was safe territory. If you needed more convincing, just watch; the next show is in ninety minutes.

I'd seen Old Faithful before. When I was fourteen, I visited Yellowstone with the family on our own road trip. My parents and brother and sister made for a jolly fivesome in a minivan. I spent much of the trip making smart-alecky remarks into the video camcorder and pretending like I had infinitely better places to be. It goes without saying that I took the experience at that age for granted. Though I like to think, in ways I wasn't fully conscious of, the memory of that trip at such a formative time had supplied an impetus for this return.

We had visited that year following the devastating fire that burned swaths of Yellowstone for months in the summer of 1988. The blaze had touched over a third of the park overall. I remember passing regions of the park charred black, where the smoke had just settled. Cecile and I and the girls were passing through on the 20th anniversary of this fire. Its effects were still present in huge sections of the park, especially on the drive heading south toward the Grand Tetons. Forests consisted of miles and miles of black and grey sticks standing in the grass, as though the fire had come through only weeks before.

But the rebirth had taken hold too. In spaces amidst these charred shells of woods, green samplings had pushed up and were now growing into strong, newly mature trees. The forest was regenerating.

We left Yellowstone and, within minutes, entered another national park, the Grand Tetons. It was the eighth national park of the journey; by summer's end we would rack up an even ten. This was only a fraction of the current total of 58 that the country officially keeps, not counting all the national monuments, memorials, historic sites, parkways and recreation areas. Wallace Stegner described the national park system, which would in turn be used prominently in the Ken Burns' documentary on the parks, as "our best idea." It could be a well-worn cliché, but the national parks are, and likely will always be, the best tangible thing about the United States. It is what brings people from all over the world. It's what brings them back.

We lingered in the quieter side of Wyoming. After the Tetons and the Shoshone National Forest, we cut through the sparsely-populated center of Wyoming, driving southeast. In the swooping valleys that connected green mountains to the brown and rugged Rocky Mountain foothills, we saw ranches that looked like kingdoms for the happiest horses alive. They roamed within miles and miles of space marked off by low fences. They could gallop all day and never cover the same ground. While these unbridled beauties flexed their muscle, the cowboys and cowhands seemed to be elsewhere. Likewise unseen, we were the inhabitants of the Wind River Indian reservation, which we crossed once the landscape flattened out and heated up. In this case, the people living on this soil seemed to need simply an escape from the unrelenting sun.

We plunked down just outside the town of Lander, small-town life perfected. The main street had a diner and a bronze statue of an American Indian astride a horse, but also a sizable used-book store and, I learned afterward, the headquarters of an indie rock label that boasted several well-known musicians, like Sufjan Stevens, who were popular back in long-lost places like Brooklyn and San Francisco's Mission District.

On the outskirts of town, the Sinks Canyon State Park offered a total vacancy at its Sawmill campground, with sites along the Popo Agie River, a river notable for the fact that it runs underground into a cavern for a quarter of a mile before reemerging. We could see only the rushing rapids. They were eerie in a way I couldn't explain because no one else was there to confirm the beauty of the scene with us.

So we confirmed this for ourselves. Julie, Louise and I stood in the swift-moving river as the sun illuminated zig-zagging mosquitoes and flecks of water splashing off the stones like tiny shooting stars before their glow vanished when the sun dropped below the canyon wall.

"Daddy, this is something incredible!" Julie announced.

"I know. It really is." Then I noticed she was looking down, not up, onto a sidepool between rocks along the bank. Water striders skated across the still surface.

"Look! These spiders are walking on the top of the water!"

- - -

Wyoming kicked up dust. Our Cruiser Royale had amassed dirt in layers. Red and brown earth had splattered the wheel wells and running boards. A dry beige coated the wheel wells and back end while the grill, hood and frontward facing plastic cabover had been painted in sooty road grime. We'd also acquired a diverse collection of the dead insects, smashed and smeared against the camper. The wings of one monstrous bug splayed out under the wipers like a permanent decal. Hosing and scrubbing down the camper in a car wash did very little. We'd wear our road dirt like a badge of honor as we entered Colorado.

At Estes Park in the Rocky Mountains, our grubby appearance allowed me to feel like the real, pioneering brand of tourist. The throngs of visitors in town, most in various plus-sizes ambling down the crowded shopped main street wearing Rockies T-shirts and eating phallic towers of ice cream. But at least, their vehicles were washed and waxed and they had showered and exfoliated that morning.

We knew better. We were hardier folk. We had camp to make and no time for the cheap baubles of tourism.

"I've always loved those old Western photos," Cecile remarked.

"What are you talking about?"

"You know, the ones where you dress up like cowboys and the take your picture, like it's the old days," she replied.

I noticed the sign over a storefront for Olde Time Western portraits. It poked holes in my veneer of authenticity.

Cecile was chasing the wild western dream again, the one created in the psyche of the foreigner. I could only relent to her request. Besides, who were we fooling?

We were escorted to the costume closet where she and the girls donned frilly dresses. I suited up in a duster, ten-gallon hat and holster with pistol and a shotgun over my shoulder for good measure. I took my position beside the faux-bar decorated with empty bottles of Jack Daniels. The photographer asked us if we were from Canada. My attempt at rootin', tootin' American had already been challenged. I now took the photo shoot seriously as the girls.

I gave the photographer our story, explaining that I grew up in Pennsylvania but we lived in France. "You picked up a little bit of a French accent sounds like," she remarked.

"Really?" I replied, adding a saloon twang to my voice. I tried to straighten my posture to show that I might have genuine cowboy blood in me somewhere and could play this part if I needed to. Any true American should know how to look like an outlaw, at the very least. Though, I wasn't nearly as convincing as the sample photos in the window or as Cecile, who grinned from ear to ear through the whole photo session, like she'd been bestowed with the actual honor of being an 19th century homesteader and the girls, her hardscrabble offspring.

We tested our mettle on the Rocky Mountain Front Range in the Moraine campground. We were joined by more old friends, Seth and Matt (known to me only as Noone and Smitty), appearing on the campground path as a hilarious sight for sore eyes.

"Wow, look at Missildine, he's got his hands full," Seth commented. Talking about someone standing beside us in the third person was the preferred method of communication among my old friends. It let conversations slip more naturally into the absurd.

"And he learned how to build a campfire," Matt teased.

"Not bad for a cheese-eating surrender monkey," Seth added in the Scottish accent of Groundskeeper Willie, old quotes from The Simpsons still tough to avoid.

"But wait, I'm a real Western outlaw." I had to defend myself. I produced the sepia photo of our festooned family and my impressive shotgun. Riotous chortling ensued over the image. "I mean, photo aside, do you think I still look like an American?"

"What?" Seth wondered if I was serious.

"Not in the picture, I'm talking in general. If you didn't know me and we were meeting for the first time at this campground tonight, where would you guess I was from?"

"I don't know," Seth said, "you never looked like you were from this country in the first place."

We added more logs and stepped in closer to the fire as the sunlight cast onto the peaks of the Rocky Mountains disappeared. Julie and Louise had gone to bed, grudgingly because as they were both enamored with the two friends who talked like their Dad.

The three of us remained standing over the fire, rather than sitting. I was too animated by the presence of old friends or feeling too protective of the lone female of the group as she sat wrapped in a blanket in the fold-out chair. We three also held a stick each in of our hands that we used to prod the dying flames. Cecile nodded off in her chair and we stayed up, lasting longer than the heat of the dark red coals.

"Why did that fire go out so quickly?"

"I don't know, Smitty, probably because of something you did."

The next day we followed Seth back into Denver, where the setting turned gritty. It had been weeks since we'd seen anything urban. With our minds still in the frontier, the drive through the never-ending suburbs of Denver was jarring. We continued on and shortly off the highway, through neighborhoods of dilapidated single-dwelling houses with liquor stores on every corner and not a person in sight. This gave way within blocks to manicured lawns and mothers pushing children in expensive strollers. Somewhere between the two, toward the center of town, off of the main drag of Colfax Ave., Seth had found a happy medium in a nice rented rowhouse.

We ate out around the corner at a Thai restaurant that evening and, afterward, spent a beautiful night sitting on Seth's stoop, with the girls asleep in his bed he offered them. We sat there covering as much conversational ground as we could before we'd have to leave here tomorrow.

"You guys aren't going to sleep yet, right?" Seth asked late into the evening. I'd never been able to turn in early around him and I wouldn't be starting now.

- - -

That morning we left not bothering to calculate or consider the distance to Cheyenne. I turned off Colfax Ave. bolstered by the loudmouth night with Seth and the late stage of the trip with over 9,000 miles on the odometer since the Hudson River Valley, enough that I simply didn't care anymore. What would be a couple hundred more miles, even if it was in the wrong direction?

I steered toward where I sensed Cheyenne might be, eschewing the map or the driving directions I failed to pay any attention to when we'd followed Seth into the city the day before. I counted on ample American signage. After fifteen minutes of no such thing, I took a left, trying my luck on a street I didn't recognize which didn't orient me in the slightest. Soon, I was making awkward three-point turns on residential streets that may have been Santa Fe as far as I knew.

"I thought you were looking for the highway?" Cecile questioned.

"Oh I am."

"Well then, let's turn around."

"I already have."

"So you're lost?"

"We'll get there."

"Do you even know what you're looking for?"

"There's a sign for Colfax again."

"Where's the map?"

"We could stay another night with Seth."

"Maybe we should have bought that GPS."
"We made it this far."
"What is the number of the highway we are looking for?"
"Don't worry I've got it under control."

As I had trusted it would, the way out of Denver popped up before I surrendered to the map. A huge sign announced I-25 North to Cheyenne. We merged with the light, early afternoon traffic and sped away before things got worse.

We were traveling north in pursuit of the Black Hills and Badlands of South Dakota that I'd insisted upon seeing. These destinations lay two days' drive away. Even once there, we'd be left with the remainder of the half of the country to cross in sufficient time, provided all went smoothly. I realized we needed, once more, to pick up the pace.

Things Freely Tossed Out of the Window of Our Moving Vehicle
* gum
* clipped fingernails
* strands of hair pulled from the bristles of a hairbrush
* banana peels
* the Wyoming "Cowboy Up" Welcome Center brochure (accidentally)
* caution (figuratively, but maybe not yet completely)
* the detailed record of trip expenses that kept our credit card balance in check (again figuratively)
* apple cores

We flew across the prairie. The plains became Great. We wound along backroads with few fellow mobile homes. After Cheyenne, a city that seemed conflicted about peddling its cowboy image to tourists, we crossed into Nebraska moving parallel to elevated railroad tracks and keeping pace with the rumbling, endless line of freight containers just above our two-lane road.

We drove until Crawford, Nebraska. We found a decent stopping point in Fort Robinson State Park, a small patch of land with rolling hills and a buffalo ranch. There, a collection of outbuildings at the old fort had a special history.

Fort Robinson was known according to the historical marker as the "outpost of the Plains," particularly during the war with the Sioux. For several decades it was the front line or, at moments, an isolated, besieged encampment in enemy territory. The cavalry eventually pushed back and prevailed.

Crazy Horse, the famed warrior, surrendered at Fort Robinson, his people having starved and many frozen to death toward the end of the long battle with the encroaching white man. He had tried to live alongside the troops in the nearby Red Cloud Indian camp until, in 1887, he was sentenced to be imprisoned at Fort Robinson and was then stabbed by a guard while trying to resist. By accounts, the fort held prisoners for two years following the death of the already legendary Crazy Horse. In 1889, a group of Cheyenne Indians staged an unsuccessful breakout and were massacred in the process. The incident came to be cited as the last of the bloodshed in the wars with the Plains Indians.

Fort Robinson was a cruelly peaceful place now. We walked to the playground. I stood over the dry grass where a swingset had been built beside a grove of trees. Louise passed a long swinging session, feet kicking higher than the horizon line, as I looked out over the flat landscape that must have provided very little in the way of hiding spots for the desperate Cheyenne fugitives.

I took a brief tour that evening of the well-preserved grounds of the fort, much of it still functional. At the lodge, where visitors can opt to sleep in the former enlisted men's quarters, I read an entry in the guestbook that praised the place for so beautifully preserving history. The visitor went on to comment that the place was also haunted and he'd seen the ghost of a soldier walking the hallway during the night. It wasn't clear if he was joking or not.

Back at our campsite, I kept the small factoid to myself and didn't stay up late alone by the fireside. Lying awake on our camper's bed, I couldn't sleep, not thinking so much about the ghosts of the white soldiers, but rather those of the Sioux and Cheyenne.

Garnishing the award for all-time trip favorite driving music was the song from Disney's Pocahontas called The Colors of the Wind. With signs of the tribal history apparent everywhere in this part of Great Plains, I again was faced with the near-impossibility of introducing my daughters to this part of American heritage simply and accurately. I'd begun backwards. Another problem was the fact that deep down, I couldn't stop myself from enjoying this version of the Pocahontas story, when taken on its own. Pocahontas urges in song, "Come run the hidden byways of the forest, come taste the sun-sweet berries of the earth, come roll in all the riches all around you, and for once never wonder what they're worth." It wasn't the worst message for kids, or adults for that matter.

But I wanted to provide the actual basics of Native American culture for them. So I purchased a Scholastic picture book from a gift shop on our way into South Dakota in the town of Hot Springs. The book was called "If You Lived with the Sioux…" and it seemed a reasonable place to introduce the history of this tribe. The book went into details of daily Sioux life and customs and the girls enjoyed having it read to them that night. I still couldn't help feeling it was written by a paleface trying hard to make amends.

It read, "The Sioux Indians believed in sharing everything they had…and there would be a kind word for anyone passing by." It sounded idyllic. Though not Disney, it was nonetheless an early reader's picture book. Toward the end, a page asked "What happened to the Sioux when the white people came?" over the image of white settlers shooting a downed buffalo. "The white people came with promises…guns….strange, new germs….whiskey…and ideas about how the Sioux should live."

All of this was, obviously, correct and the book handled a delicate issue for young readers with balance. Still, there was a tinge of swayed objectivity running through the text, one that usually crept in whenever the ancestors of the guilty parties tackled issues that met at a crossroads of culture, politics, race and inequality.

"Where are the Indians now?" Julie asked after I finished.

"They are still here. They dress and drive cars and do things just like everyone else does. They don't wear feathered headdresses as much anymore."

"That's too bad," Julie said crestfallen.

"No, it's...yes, it's a little bit too bad. But it's alright. It's better, in the end." She caught my uncertainty.

We'd visited a museum back in Wyoming with displays of the local tribes, though it hadn't left much of an impression. For further instruction, we stopped briefly at the Crazy Horse Memorial.

The monument to Native American Plains heritage started construction in 1948, and sixty years later, still features only the carved profile of the proud warrior. Evidently, a new demolition was planned for the coming fall. Unsure if anything about the head of Crazyhorse struggling to emerge from a mountainside was at all meaningful, we pushed on. Its location was fairly arbitrary, as Crazy Horse had requested to keep the site of his a burial a secret so he'd never be found by white men. The only real reason construction had started here was in response to the four other famous heads carved into the Black Hills several miles north.

Mount Rushmore, we soon confirmed, had been fully completed.

The Lakota people had inhabited the Black Hills and were promised this land. But after defeat in the Sioux Wars, they were summarily and permanently forced off. Several decades later the likenesses of George Washington, Thomas

Jefferson, Theodor Roosevelt and Abraham Lincoln were blasted and chiseled into the mountainside.

The history notwithstanding, I wasn't sure I'd even allow Mt. Rushmore all that much grandeur. The monument is four busts perched on a medium-sized ridge that are significantly less towering and impressive than I expected them to be, particularly when taken in view of the mountain that stops abruptly at the left.

At first glance, I thought the faces represented a mock-up of the real Mt. Rushmore, located somewhere else. But this was the thing, an image reproduced so often the original is an inevitable letdown. I preferred the view from the highway winding toward the monument, where you can see the profile of Washington, his back to the wall like he's trying to make himself inconspicuous. But no such luck.

The stone heads get the full tourist treatment, with a huge viewing area, a state flag-adorned colonnade, an audio tour, a small museum about the construction, two films and two separate gift shops. The audio tour has recently added Lakota to the language options, a move that rang with the best of intentions.

We stayed to snap several pictures, like all other visitors. We learned about the monument's megalomaniacal sculptor, Gutzon Borglum, and his large-scale techniques and watched one of the films that concerned the surrounding nature and wildlife of the Black Hills.

Afterward, we took one more picture for good measure, asking a friendly and wisecracking family from Minnesota to get the four of us together, in turn doing the same for them. We watched a Boy Scout troop trudge across the colonnade. Like them, we'd come because it was there and because we could confirm this afterward to others who hadn't gone all the way to verify this fact.

Then we noticed bikers. Every other person at Mt. Rushmore, after I started counting, was clad in bandanas, leather and tight jeans. Of vehicles in the parking lot, an entire level was filled with Harley-Davidson motorcycles.

There was a one-word explanation for this: Sturgis.

At Mt. Rushmore, and in all the towns within a hundred mile radius, we heard the steady growl of motorcycle engines. Starting back in Cheyenne we had noticed an inordinate two-wheeled presence. At stops approaching the Black Hills, most restaurants and hotels had signs out that said "Riders Welcome." Before we were informed, we wondered "Who's riding?"

Annually, the otherwise sleepy town of Sturgis, South Dakota holds one of the world's largest motorcycle rallies. The event began as a motor club's get together, but now the average attendance surpasses the population of the state the event is held in. Tricked-out bikes overran the town of Keystone, the ad hoc village of Rushmore miles from Sturgis. We walked down the main street of Keystone with its old-west style shops and saloons. Instead of horses hitched to a post, the sidewalk was lined with rows of chrome and steel shimmering in the afternoon sun.

In another life, and maybe with a more imposing physical build, I could have been a biker. Wade, back in York, had recently purchased a Triumph. "The kind Dylan crashed in," he'd remarked during my visit, after throwing open the doors to his shed. The bike had been waiting there silently, a silver and black invitation to all the places you weren't really supposed to go.

I'd ridden a motorcycle once in my life, when my father-in-law let me take his smaller cycle for a spin around his property. I proceeded to drive his machine through a row of his neatly trimmed hedges. A life fuel-injected on two wheels wasn't for me. But still looking at my friend's Triumph early in our trip, and then much later finding myself in Keystone witnessing the spectacle of the Sturgis pilgrimage, I could hear the raucous call that brought these people together, even if I'd probably never heed it.

Richard La Plante in his book, Detours, about his trip to Sturgis, summed up the scene during the rally week as "Power and strength. Desire and sexuality."

We saw plenty of this, even well outside its epicenter. Men and women sported as little of the leather and bandana as they could in order to showcase monstrous tattoos, rippling muscles or silicon-pumped breasts while parading up and down streets and in and out of bars, swigging from open beer bottles at midday.

We tried to blend in wearing baggy T-shirts and shorts holding tightly to Julie's and Louise's hands, not sure if we were allowed to pass freely among this crowd, but nonetheless curious. We stopped for ice cream. As the girls sat at a storefront bench, polishing off their cones with the rapt intensity reserved only for this food, I noticed a woman in an all-black leather jumpsuit taking pictures of Julie and Louise. She picked up on my suspicion.

"They're adorable," she smiled. She showed me the hi-res digital closeup she'd taken, with perfect lighting on their hair and faces. "I can send you these photos if you want."

She was with her husband, having traveled from Illinois. She was an older woman, even possibly of age to be a grandmother, but was trim and obviously fit enough to handle several hundred miles riding in the open saddle of a Harley.

"So what goes on once you get to Sturgis?" I asked her.

"Plenty I wouldn't recommend taking the kids to."

She was friendlier than could ever have been expected, and more easygoing than most RVers. Several weeks later, this woman did indeed email me the gorgeous studio-like digital portraits of the girls.

The Sturgis crowd looked menacing at first glance, but the more we gawked from the bench, the more we saw an element of sincerity and goodwill. As La Plante described it, "Sturgis was like entering a different society, with a different set of values and customs. I met heart surgeons and pawn brokers, grandmas and preachers, but without the façade of money and status my interaction was at a personal level with no ulterior motives."

Walking back to the camper, Louise bumped into the leg of a gigantic bearded man in a jean vest and wraparound shades. He scowled and looked down at what must have felt like a barely detectable breeze brushing up against him. The man's expression softened and he removed his sunglasses.

"Oh, excuse me, darlin'," the biker said, craning downward to Louise. She grinned up at him like she'd just made a friend who happened to be eleven times her size.

Surrounded by these so-called renegades and bullies I never felt in any kind of danger. Perhaps with the strength and aggression on unabashed display in the hardbodies of the bikes and in the riders themselves, there was no room for suspicion and therefore no mistrust.

I wanted to visit the nearby town of Deadwood, mainly because of the HBO series that depicted the frontier town's transition from lawlessness to order, but figured we'd had enough. The scene at that historic gambling town of Wild Bill Hickok and Calamity Jane probably turned more raw and R-rated, with these new rowdy denizens on their mechanized horses. We'd already needed to swing wide and shield the girl's eyes when passing the Red Garter Saloon in Keystone that afternoon.

Instead, we settled into a campsite two miles from Rushmore at Horsethief Lake. At least, the name felt dangerous.

"You think we should trade in the RV for a shiny new hog?" I inquired with Cecile.

"If I remember correctly, you don't know how to ride a motorcycle?"

"Oh, right."

"Also we're renting this RV."

"The girls could ride in a sidecar."

"Louise needs to have her diaper changed, again." Cecile reminded me. "Nevermind, actually, I'll do that. But can you do a fire? We need to finish the hot dogs we have left."

"Look at you, you've become fully domesticated."

She squinted back at me. "Are you about to tell me you're going to join a motorcycle gang?"

It was an idea worth entertaining for a few more hours. Well, after dinner and before I went to bed, I heard the throbbing engines of motorcycles coming around the mountain bend and one of the riders hooting to the night sky to reassure everyone that the wild west had not yet been fully tamed.

"Can we go back to where we were yesterday?" Julie asked during the driving reverie heading due east straight through South Dakota.

"Where's that, sweetpea? Mount Rushmore? The mountain with the presidents, you mean?"

"No, the place with the white sand."

"The white sand desert? That wasn't yesterday!"

"I mean before yesterday."

"The place called White Sands was more than a month ago, Julie."

"Ok, but can we go back there?"

"That was just a month?" Cecile chimed in. "Wowie, it feels like a year."

The girls traveled with their own mental map and an internal clock that had little relation to the one their parents relied on. The days and sights that accompanied them had started to mix with the unreliable calendar that memory provided us. I wasn't certain how many days, weeks or months had passed between the Southwest and the horseshoe we'd made to get from there to the Great Plains. We conceived of time with the minds of children, where its passage was no longer linear but performed fantastic loops and somersaults. I couldn't immediately recall how long we'd been on the road. It could have been a year or two. Or maybe just a long weekend.

For another perspective on time that we were increasingly short on, we could go geologic, where, for instance, the Badlands were disappearing before our eyes. According to the general info at this national park, east of the Black Hills, the thin spires and jagged ridges of sediment in the Badlands are a result of deposition and erosion. The layers of this process are exposed in the colorful bands like they've been applied in brushstrokes by a fastidious master painter. The movements have uncovered a wealth of fossils, making this a hotspot for paleontologists. With this erosion, the Badlands are disappearing at a rate of one inch per year and in another few hundred thousand, a single breath in the life of the planet, these lonely, beautiful sandcastles rising out of the prairie will have returned to a flat floodplain.

We'd been given the chance to catch them before they go. *Les mauvaises terre à traverser*, as the French explorers first described it, were especially mauvaise and strange given their abrupt appearance in the otherwise gently swaying plains of the region. From the top of the one of ridges, we watched the Midwest changing guard with the west over a landscape alternating between craggy, ghostly peaks and swaying green grass.

We parked ourselves for the night at a campground. At sunset, the girls played with a nearby tetherball. Cecile and I shared a picnic table bench facing a pink and violet light cast across the underbelly of the clouds. The silhouettes of a trio of horseback riders rose over the horizon.

"Let's get married," Cecile proposed to me this time, the light from the sky on her face.

"Already did."

"Shoot, that's right. You mean, we can't do it all again?"

"I think they don't let you do that. But we could try."

But we wouldn't escape without some of the bad. As I was coming back into the camper the next morning, I slid the side door open, not seeing that Louise was, at that moment, leaning against the tinted windows. She tumbled out, clanging the back of her head on the running board.

Here was another painful spill for her, in what was becoming a particularly accident-prone trip for this resilient two-year-old. Because I had now watched Louise absorb one injury too many, because we'd been up the night before slapping at blood-thirsty mosquitoes, because we were now leaving the grand west, because we'd tempted harm's way enough, I declared that we leave the untamed west as soon as possible.

On the unbending highway 90, we were passed on the left by Sturgis riders most of whom who looked hungover and much wearier than we were.

I switched on the radio, having listened to all our tapes four or five times. I stopped on a Christian radio broadcast. The host was discussing with one of his callers the hazards of letting your Christian child go off to a secular university, where they will encounter ungodly temptation.

"College can be a true test of one's faith in the Lord," the host reminded the caller. I certainly agreed, as I'd failed that test with flying colors on a combination of spirited hedonism, grunge music, kind and open-minded atheist friends and the gradual realization that the world was more complex than my church youth group had lead me to believe.

I'd started as a Presbyterian. I was still on the church rolls of the First Presbyterian Church of York, in fact, though I hadn't been back there since our wedding four years ago and even then it was more a sentimental choice and not a deep-faith, God's blessing kind of wedding. Since it was Cecile's second marriage and since Julie was already ten months old when we'd gotten hitched, we'd taken a path that most Christians don't.

But between that point and high school, the dangerous college years the radio host was by now tossing scripture and blanket statements over, I'd come to broaden my view. I'd reached the reasonable conclusion that there are no conclusions.

Though I hadn't abandoned spirituality altogether either. I still believed in prayer, but at the place where it intersected with meditation. I still believed in some manifestation of god, but now where it met with a wider divinity expanded to include the living things on Earth.

College, and then California and then France, might have shaken me agnostic. But I'd held onto a sense of faith. Whatever my disagreements with the pastors who'd influenced me, including my very own grandfather, and no matter my break with a church community, I held a place in my mind and spirit for faith. Like riding a bike, I'd never lost the ability to believe in something higher, greater. This early practice of faith had allowed me to transfer faith elsewhere: a faith in loved ones, a faith that the world is lurching clumsily toward good and a faith in things I'm still only able to name as miracles and can't resign myself to label as coincidence.

With our voyage end in view, I realized the luck we'd had on the road, the lack of serious accidents, almost unfailingly good weather and the small surprises wherever our camper stopped. It had come together because of a mixture of planning, patience, resourcefulness and flexibility. But some part of had to come thanks to a kind of grace.

The next day Louise was still talking about her boo-boo ("bou-bou" in French). She pointed to the bump on her head and winced.

"I'm sure it's nothing," I turned to Cecile.

"Yeah, I know."

"I mean, if it was something, we'd know, right?"

"Nothing."

"You're thinking we should check it out?"

"But it's nothing, probably."

We both sat silent for a full minute while worst-case scenarios crept into our heads.

"We should check it out, right?"

"Yes, we should."

We found the Mercy Medical Center ER in Sioux City, Iowa, over the South Dakota border.

It turned out Louise was fine. A series of brief tests verified that she'd merely suffered another bump and that, like all two-year olds, she was tougher than we gave her credit for. Louise remained patient and pleased with the amount of attention she was suddenly receiving from five adults in the room. The nurses and doctor were attentive. So was the financial planner who sat down longer than anyone of them with us, to discuss payment plans like we were taking out a bank loan.

"We'll just pay this now and all of it will be reimbursed by our French coverage," I said.

"Really?" the hospital financial planner looked at us dumbfounded. I pulled out my green Carte Vitale, the French universal health card that had all our family's medical records stored in its smart chip. The financial planner grew frightened.

After the hospital visit, we all agreed on the comforts of the Holiday Inn Express beckoning us from the highway. The hotel was quiet, clean and spacious and we had the indoor pool all to ourselves. Everyone slept well that night in our two double beds.

I bunked, as usual, with Louise. While she sucked her thumb and dreamed, I lay awake beside her as the glare from an illuminated streetlamp seeped in from behind drawn curtains.

Beside A Sleeping Daughter
* why does her face looks so serious and mature when her eyes are closed?
* what will I do when she's too big to curl up into a ball beside me?
* what will I do when the sound of her sucking her thumb is no longer there to remind me that she's okay?
* what am going to do next year?
* we could always bring another human being like this into the world
* is Louise maybe, on a subconscious level, reading my mind?
* how do she and her sister manage to breathe out miracles for us everyday?
* how do I continue to take them for granted?
* how was I ever deemed worthy of the unending, bone-wearying job of making sure they stick around to perform them?
* am I the only person who sees them as miracles?
* am I still really an agnostic?

- - -

We were returning now, getting back all over the place. We were coming in from the harsher lands of the west and into the populated fold. We could see the short gap between here and the return dot on our map. We were starting to feel like we'd been here before. We were in Iowa.

In Iowa, the temptation to pick a small town and begin unloading the camper there for a new life as a farmer or even a friendly claims adjuster was clear and present. Though it has a reputation as a landlocked and corn-fed Midwestern nowheresville, anyone with any connection with the place seemed to be hopelessly in love with Iowa. It has taken on the properties of myth without anyone noticing, where the residents of River City sing to Professor Harold Hill in The Music Man "Wouldn't you like to give Iowa a try?" and the ghost of Shoeless Joe Jackson in Field of Dreams asks "Is this heaven?" to which the reply comes "No, it's Iowa." Famous author and world traveler Bill Bryson has remarked on several occasions that there is nowhere in the world quite like his home state.

As we headed toward Des Moines, the truth behind Iowa's praise spread over broad hills and corn silos. There wasn't much to it, which was the idea. There wasn't much. We were not goaded by any world-famous attractions, monuments or swelling urban centers. Iowa was deliberately going about being a solid state of the union without the fanfare. It superseded the idea of American heartland as a cliché. It felt like a source of the steady pulse of the country, yet undisturbed by any of the looming problems of the rest of the country. The soft, fertile landscape around us became a kind of cradle.

Generations before me, on both sides of my family, had settled in Iowa. A large portion of them were buried in Ames, just north of the capital Des Moines. Was it this connection that made me feel instantly at home here?

Beside wholesomeness, waiting for us in Des Moines was the fair. I turned into a giddy man-child as we crossed the gates into the main thoroughfare of the 2008 Iowa State

Fair. On the left, flag-adorned stands lined the street leading to the outdoor stadium and, on the right, the world's largest choice of food for sale that a person can consume while standing. My legs walked me, without thought, toward a single stand that sold hot wings, jalapeno poppers, lemon shake-ups, fresh onion rings, pulled pork barbeque, fries, giant ½ tenderloin and, like every vendor at this fair, corn dogs.

"Let's stay all week," I whispered to Cecile.

"Or until five-thirty," she tried to calm me down.

We skipped over to the rides, figuring we'd dizzy ourselves first and then eat following. While Julie ventured onto her first roller coaster, Louise tried a game of hooking plastic ducks with the fishing line. Coming up empty, the lady working the booth told Louise to select a plush toy anyway.

We toured the farm show pavilion. Prize-winning horses, pigs and cows proudly chewed on straw beside their blue ribbons. Soft young calves didn't mind the barrage of tiny hands stroking and patting their heads. I watched while finding, again by accident, a pulled pork barbeque sandwich in my hand. I tried, in vain, to finish it off before Cecile noticed.

By the stables, we ran into the 2008 state fair queen, Ashley Quade, while simultaneously looking at the largest bull I'd ever seen in my life. Somehow the two together, a champion bull the size of a Jeep, and the reed-thin crowned queen threw me off for a second.

My daughters, of course, only had eyes for the queen. The sight of the fair queen still in sash and sparkling tiara made Julie swoon. A real-life Cinderella had arrived expressly to meet her. The queen in turn was instantly drawn to Julie. She asked her if she would like to be in a pageant one day too, affirmative answer implied. Miss Quade assured Julie that she would make a great queen to which Julie nodded, too dazzled to speak. This was symbiotic relationship; Julie provided the adulation and the Fair queen provided the vision, each of them completing the other's shared fantasy.

Not all Iowans were dainty teen beauty pageant winners. The majority of the fair visitors were on the other side of the weight scale. The standard look was hefty with faces like large thumbs but smiles that were jolly without being insipid. Almost every one of them, also, wore at minimum one item of clothing with the words "Iowa" on it. Whether an Iowa State hat or a University of Iowa tee, a prerequisite had been established that, as a due for living in this bucolic utopia, you had to walk around advertising for it.

I talked with a friendly woman sitting near us in a yellow "Beat State" shirt at the outdoor picnic tables as I worked my way through, not one but two corn dogs, and some fresh-squeezed lemonade. I told her how much we loved the area and I mentioned my family history, with my relatives buried north of here in Ames and how my great-grandfather would, each year, show off farming equipment at the fair. It made me want to live here, I told her.

After hearing my praises she said humbly that, "I'd've thought things would be better over there in Paris."

"Well, you'd be surprised what you can find in your own backyard too," I told her. Though maybe it was time I start showing pride for the culture I lived in. I should have been wearing a tricolor France shirt this whole time. For now, I settled on one with a Hawkeye that I picked up on the way out.

With dinner thrown off by the non-stop eating we'd done all day and the girl's both asleep in either an evening nap or early bedtime, we kept driving, through the whole eastern half of the state until we reached Iowa City. We'd settled for another hotel, having lost our camplust almost entirely by now. Oddly, the first four places we tried had no vacancy. We tried the pricier Marriot, which had one room remaining.

"Is there a convention going on here?" Cecile asked at the Marriot desk.

"No," the woman behind the counter politely corrected, "many of our guests are currently long-stay."

She paused, checking to see if we understood why. Registering our still quizzical looks, she added, "A lot of people lost their houses in the flood."

She referred to the flood that had hit Cedar Rapids. In June, the Cedar River that envelops the city had risen to 31 feet and washed over an area of ten square miles. According to estimates I later read, some 18,000 people had been displaced. Two months later we were seeing the result. I looked around the lobby and saw people in their socks lounging on couches and gabbing about their day. A mother and daughter waited by the elevator with a load of folded laundry. These people weren't coming or going anywhere. This was their home for now. And they were among the lucky ones.

So Iowa wasn't set apart from the problems of the rest of the world after all. The extreme weather that seemed more common each year, climate change or not, raged in these parts too. The country was still feeling the effects of the massive displacement and unmitigated tragedy from Hurricane Katrina in New Orleans. Three years later, by the Mississippi Delta, empty pre-fab trailers still sat idle waiting for government bureaucracy to clear their usage, while thousands remained homeless. Here in Iowa City, the ruin was on a much smaller scale. Still, there was an eerie mood; the hotel felt like part shelter. The woman behind the desk took on the air of a caretaker, her manner neither overly cheery nor dour.

"So where are you folks from?" she then asked, not rushing to change the subject, just undeterred in her habit of considering warmth a matter of routine.

- - -

I'd also watched Iowa in the news that January prior, when it was the first to signal something big was happening that year in the Democratic party.

From across the Atlantic, I'd tuned in online to the presidential election like it was a mini-series. In early 2008, I'd become convinced that Barack Obama stood as the more capable candidate, who also happened to be the more agile politician. It helped that his ideas also made infinitely more sense to me, but that was another discussion.

But once back on the actual soil at stake, I wasn't so sure. After moving through small-towns in Virginia, Alabama, Oklahoma, Idaho, Wyoming and South Dakota, my doubt had mushroomed. How would Obama bridge the cultural differences some of these regions represented? Did these communities want to even listen? What did it say about both of the major political parties when the most frequent political signage we saw in rural areas everywhere was "Ron Paul for President," the perennial dark horse.

More than a few people, whether pulling for Obama or not, said what a lot of pundits never stated directly. "This country won't elect a black president."

A man in a local paper in Pennsylvania was quoted before the state's Democratic primary as saying he would never vote for him because "His name is Barack Hussein Obama. Period."

An old high school friend back in Pennsylvania had declared, "He lost my vote when he said he listened to that rapper Ludacris."

Another woman in the New Mexico campground on the 4th of July had mentioned that she wouldn't vote for someone who had so many international ties. In what I sensed was a careful guarding of her words, she simply added, "I don't get overseas so much, what with all the meanness." This was her nonconfrontational way of saying she wouldn't be voting for far-out ideas.

In Peekskill, New York, at the camper rental lot, we talked with a man, taking fewer pains to hide his true stripes, who said, "If he wins, all the blacks will riot."

"What if he loses?" I asked.

"Oh, they'll probably riot then too."

My mother had related a story of some Obama volunteers she knew at the university where she worked who'd gone house-to-house in the suburbs of Lancaster, PA. At one house, an older woman took one look at the Obama '08 gear and said "Don't you know that man's going to enslave the white race?"

"In no other country in the world is my story even possible," Obama himself proclaimed in his stump speech. It was a crucial point he'd made hundreds of times, summing up his life story. It highlighted the essential difference he represented as a candidate, while also laying claim to his utter Americanness. Despite all the prejudice and mistrust he faced, his line still held true.

In France, they took this claim as an affront. On French cable news, I watched a three-hour roundtable discussion, the sort designed never to reach any conclusions, over this question. Could France elect a black candidate with a strange name, they wondered? The closest thing to a consensus, on that program, and on most others in the country was: non.

Our camper rolled toward Chicago where the Obama campaign was fast at work on extinguishing the doubt of the nation. But we hadn't come for politics or to search for a new wave of hope or change emanating from this city. We'd come, once more, for old friends, to catch and meet their one-year old son.

From their neighborhood called Ukrainian Village in western Chicago we ventured downtown to Millennium Park, where in less than three months I'd watch CNN International as the first black president of the country walked out onto the main stage to give a victory speech. The supporters, and a healthy majority of the country, would be overjoyed.

On this sunny August day, downtown Chicago seemed to be already coursing with the energy that would drive citizens to that moment. In this newly-landscaped park, we mixed in with the flurry of activities open to the public. We stopped at a toy block-building area and an origami crafts table, then watched a teenage dance troupe perform choreographed moves. Later, we stepped barefoot into the Crown Fountain, where massive photographed portraits smiled and spat water out at the diverse crowd getting their feet wet. We all took our picture beside the large, odd silver bean that reflected the downtown skyscrapers on its surface.

Though I wished I could stay to share the buzz of the place, we needed to leave Chicago before rush hour. We said goodbye with the repeated promise to spend more time together at a later date, one which none of us were sincerely certain would come.

We hit Indiana. The end crept toward us. The expanses of the west and the places of big shoulders had begun to gather up what might be left of my nostalgia and my need to stay. I couldn't be sure I'd ever see them again or that I'd ever feel the need to.

SAVE FOR FIREFLIES

EAST - - -

Green and white interstate signs announced South Bend, Michigan City and Elkhart. We decided after dinner that we'd continue on through the night, despite the one working headlight on the camper we never did take the maintenance day to address.

Out of the darkness then, a giant sign lit by klieg lights welcomed us to Ohio, The Heart of It All, and shortly after the first toll road we'd encountered on the entire trip, the Ohio Turnpike. From there signs flashed Holiday City, Wauseon and 120 miles to Cleveland. We drove through Toledo, though I never recalled seeing it. By the time I reached Sandusky, the red brakes lights ahead of me and the zooming white to my left blurred with the glow of my speedometer. The orange gaslight blipped on among them. "I should stop," I croaked to the others, fast asleep in their seats.

I pulled into a gas station at the exit that led toward the legendary amusement park Cedar Point. We found a place behind the station in the shadows, where an eighteen-wheeler had parked for the night, engine still running.

"This is where we're stopping?" Cecile woke.

"It'll be one of our last nights in the camper. We might as well make it... memorable."

Cecile and I took turns using the gas station bathroom. As she returned, she closed the camper curtains and locked the doors.
"The keys are in the ignition right?"
"Yes."
"Can you do just one more thing?"
"What's that?"
"Stop worrying so much."
"It's not me doing the worrying."
"Okay, good."
"Besides I know this area. People are nice in Ohio. I was a kid around here once."

After finishing grad school, my dad accepted an editor's job at the Lorain Morning Journal, a daily newspaper in this working-class town on Lake Erie, a half-hour west of Cleveland. He and his wife and their twelve-month old baby son eventually settled into a house in the Lakeview neighborhood, within walking distance of a small public beach. The son grew up, taking up residence in the top floor of the house after the attic was renovated where he had some space away from his younger brother and his baby sister, who'd also, in the meantime, entered the household.

The view onto the neighborhood from the attic, perched among the sycamores that lined the street, was, at the time, the highest height on the planet. But the biggest draw was the beach, where summers were whiled away digging holes in the sand that almost reached China. If only the sun hadn't dropped below the park's trees and his mom hadn't announced it was time to go, he could have reached the foundation of the Great Wall.

Then, one morning on the waning half of 2008, twenty-four years after I'd last set foot on this sand, I returned to see that my holes to China had been filled.

I walked toward the water with Julie. She made footprints in the sand that had just been smoothed by maintenance crews. The beach was half the size I remembered, ending at the lake in less than ten full paces, where it used to be a vast desert landscape. The sun was bright enough to make the lighthouse in the distance nearly washed out into invisibility. At my feet, the freshwater lapped in waves the size of curled hands onto the shore. Having come all this way, there hadn't been a sight yet that carried the same magnitude as this little strip of beach.

It was once the shore from which all water and oceans began and from which the land behind me represented a perilous, fantastic unknown. Having returned now from that unknown, I realized in my dreaming mind I still viewed Lakeview Beach as square one. It was the undisputed center of the world, the point from which everything else fanned out forever.

Having left it, but revisited again and again in memory, this actual, in person return packed a wallop of cognitive shock. It wasn't just a dream. These buildings, these trees and this sand actually existed and had continued to exist long after I'd left it. It was greater than me.

Was it merely because this stop fell as our nation-wide search was coming to a close? Or because we'd been more or less adrift for months? Standing there, it dawned on me that it wasn't only the past five years in France that I'd never felt like I belonged. My restlessness, my rootlessness had begun years before. I hadn't truly belonged in ages. We'd left Lake Erie when I was ten. I was back now grabbing at fleeting moments of summer. I was back ready to restart my digging through to the other side of the earth.

The reality instead was that I'd dug and dug and made it all the way to France, to a woman and two Franco-American daughters I now couldn't be without. Wild and ridiculous fantasies tend to come true more often than we're willing to admit. So be careful what you wish for. In fact, the better advice is to be much more careless in your wishful thinking.

And not stake down home to a small, static patch of the globe.

When The Lists Begin to Inform the Travelogue
* you drove a little fast
* and missed some amazing places
* you also should have taken more time to talk to people
* and sought out more strangers
* in fact, you could write an entire second book with the things you've left out
* but you certainly spent a lot of time on food
* you can't forget the time you opted for dinner at a chain restaurant while you had a cooler full of fresh vegetables
* maybe there's a career move for you there somewhere
* you also may have reserved the real moments of truth for lists
* what's in between could turn into a mere fantasy

* does that mean it still counts?
* does that mean it has a singular message?
* or that you've figured out America?
* you can try to keep writing this tale forever but you'll only fall further away from the critical purpose in taking it

As for the reality of the city of Lorain, Ohio in 2008, I couldn't ignore the flip side of my daydreaming. Lorain had seen tough times before and always endured as a working-class city, known for its steel mills and car assembly plant. Recently it had followed the economic trajectory of the rest of the country with high unemployment and plummeting home prices. Old friends my parents kept in touch with described the rapidly declining public schools, where the high school I would have attended if we stayed had, a year ago, shut its doors forcing two schools to merge into one.

The overcrowded, underfunded school system then made more cuts, like the elimination of almost all extracurricular activities. Meanwhile, the general lack of public funds meant problems elsewhere. The county prison, for one, couldn't be maintained, so convicted criminals were being sentenced and then immediately released with no place to hold them. My father's old newspaper still published a paper on a daily basis but faced grave revenue problems as more readers migrated online.

These problems were not isolated only to the Rust Belt, but nonetheless were felt with a familiar sting in Lorain. I was lucky to have visited Lakeview Beach, which unlike any other public space in Lorain, had that year become a part of the state-funded Metroparks system. The beach and surrounding park appeared clean and well-groomed, a shining gem in otherwise gray times. I hoped, as I left again too soon, that the people could build from this small shore.

We took the 90 at the 80/90 split through Cleveland, following the northeasterly curve of Lake Erie. We entered Pennsylvania, cutting through the northwestern corner that stuck up like a cottage chimney on the state, before reaching New York. We'd now clocked in well over 11,000 miles of driving. We'd crossed 32 different states.

Cecile's eating of asphalt had been accomplished. We'd found a rhythm of movement that not only suited the four of us by now, but that we woke up each morning longing for. She and I on the trip, as in so many other aspects of our life together, had unconsciously grown around the wants and desires of one another.

I wanted a story to tell. She wanted motion. As I scribbled out the experiences of the trip, this writing mimicked the marathon pulse of the travel she'd craved. My sentences had formed around Cecile's vision of a swiftly-traveled arc, my words rolled off my pen like the white dotted line in the road and paragraphs broke like the nightly pauses in this far, shared hurtle.

My parents waited at Lake Chautauqua at the Chautauqua Institution, where they were staying for the week. They greeted us, like before, with the surprise joy that we'd managed to show up again. My sister, along with friends of the family and a large dinner table spread, welcomed us inside. I explained to them that I was having trouble remembering all we'd just seen, but that morning we'd stopped at the most precious little lakeside town whose name they'd never guess.

Aside from the warmth of family, we were at another unique place. The Chautauqua Institution has created something difficult to find anywhere else in the country. Along Lake Chautauqua in Western New York State, it is a community, founded by Methodists but now loosely interfaith, that for nine weeks becomes a tribute to arts, music, spirituality and, chiefly, education. A kind of a midsize liberal arts college for all ages, the grounds of the Institution hold a library, an outdoor amphitheater and Victorian houses and hotels. During the summer, studies are on offer for everyone, a symphony performs three times a week, multiple religious services are held and speakers give lectures and talks twice daily around a weekly theme. For more than a hundred years, this annual thinking vacation has been taking place.

It is also a gated community that requires a pass to enter. Taking advantage of the programs isn't cheap. The Institution describes itself as fostering an open and congenial atmosphere, which is theoretically and individually true. The people of Chautauqua mean well. Though, their openness is not instantly on display. Those who take up residence here for the summer are often the slowest to say hello along the walking paths. The lectures, at times, pander to the crowd by proudly reinforcing safe, long-held and traditionally liberal beliefs. But, like most liberals, these people are trying; they want to learn and they want to listen.

My foursome, however, had arrived to Chautauqua not so much to enrich, but to decompress. Feeling proud of myself for having completed our trip, I had wrongly expected everyone to express an unending fascination with our adventures. "I can't wait to hear all the stories," several people said, though the moment to recount them never really came.

I uploaded hundreds of pictures taken on the road into an online photo gallery. I turned to my parents the next evening and said, "Hey, would you like to look at all of our trip photos?" They both looked at each other hesitantly. "Uh...sure, okay, I just want to do this one thing first," my Mom said. I had become the annoying travel slideshow guy.

After Chautauqua, we stopped again for an overnight with my friend Wade, back through PA and back to York, who we'd seen at the beginning of the summer. His wife announced this time that they'd be having another baby, due that spring. Families and communities kept growing.

Wade meanwhile was readying for a new school year at the high school, presiding over English classes in one of my old homerooms. Staring at the final bend of our trip, I envied his position slightly again. If only I hadn't kept bouncing around all over the world and stayed with my roots instead. If only I'd stuck with the people who had more to offer than I'd given them credit for during my teenage years. I mentioned this to Wade.

"Yeah, but then you're stuck in the same place," he commented with an exasperated look on his face. It was simple to idealize the road we'd both not taken.

Back in Lancaster for the final goodbye, Cecile wanted to tour Amish country. We took the back roads through Bird-in-Hand one evening on the way to a traditional Pennsylvania Dutch restaurant.

As my Dad drove the six of us, we drove by Amish farmlands, the barns and buildings easily identifiable by the lack of electrical and telephone wires running into the homes. The schoolhouses were still one-room. The cows were still milked by hand and the fields plowed by horse. Black buggies scooted along the shoulder of the busy four lane roads, often with a small black bonnet peeking over the open back window.

My mom pointed out the new fences around the schoolhouses, constructed after the school shooting that left five Amish children dead in the community of Nickel Mines. Though merely a shoulder high fence that may or not have even included a lock, it represented a step for the Amish toward acknowledging the intrusion of the modern world.

Change creeps into the Amish community, some as reaction to the excess of contemporary life, as it's been created by "the English" (the Amish word for the rest of us). Other change manifests in the accretion of modern tools in sustaining livelihood. Merchants and businessmen in the Pennsylvania Dutch communities now typically use calculators and computers that they refer as "business-helping machines."

The Amish have also created a booming tourism industry in Lancaster County. Again, like the bawdy names Intercourse and Blue Ball, it's a matter of debate whether the Amish encourage the money that tourists bring in or whether they find it disconcerting. Stores all along Lancaster's main artery Rt. 30 advertise Amish goods and trinkets. Sit-down restaurants of all stripes offer authentic Amish cuisine. Package tours for weekenders coming in from New York and New Jersey abound.

The Good 'N Plenty Restaurant in Bird-in-Hand is off the main roads but no less popular. Though the gift shop and bus parking may have pointed to a place whose authenticity was long ago lost to tourism, the restaurant is still run by its Pennsylvania Dutch founders, Christ and Dolly Lapp, and their extended family. If the shared plates and the long cafeteria-style tables didn't convince patrons, the food did.

I ate there as if I was a growing teen at my grandmother's house for the Sunday brunch of egg noodles and fried chicken. Once I pushed away from my place setting, vowing to eat nothing but salads until the end of our trip, the server swooped in with three types of pie.

The next night, still stuffed, we took in a minor league baseball game to watch the Lancaster Barnstormers face the Newark Bears. This rounded out the requisite American experiences better than any major league baseball game. The stadium and the Barnstormer fans exhibited everything that was right about baseball that the majors lately seemed to be getting wrong: a sense of hometown spirit and an emphasis on younger fans who could feel like they belonged. Our girls watched for a full inning, before skipping off to the playground and bouncy castle situated beyond the outfield.

Cecile, however, stayed to stare at the field. Cecile's longtime favorite movie is The Natural. I've only ever partially understood why. I left her to fantasize that Robert Redford was warming up on deck for Lancaster.

I struck up a conversation with my Dad, a baseball game being one of the best places to chew the fat over completely unrelated topics with your father. During the course of the conversation, the prospect of having a third kid came up. I explained that it wasn't final yet, but that we'd probably be sticking with two. I mentioned the added work of a third. Then, countering my own argument, I noted to him, "But, you guys did a great job with three."

"We did?" my Dad questioned, pleasantly surprised. "Thank you." He was joking, but still showed notable relief at my positive feedback. Of course, they'd done an amazing job- everyday for the past thirty-three years had been evidence of that. But parents, no matter the age, are somehow never as certain of their abilities as they let on.

Cecile and I went to the movies. On the way there, the back half of the camper echoed, conspicuously empty, the girls left with their grandparents.

"What happens now? I mean, when we land back in France?" I asked.

"Oh, don't think about it so much."

"What about your new job opportunity in Paris?"

"I don't know. I keep going over it in my head."

"Oh you mean, you're thinking?"

"The important part is not me. A job comes and goes."

"I wish I could be a stay-at-home Dad expat for life."

"You've still got a few more years working for the two big bosses."

"Right, soon they're teenagers and it's tattoos and Facebook accounts."
"Don't make me think of this."
"Yes, we should probably just slow down. We have time. A little, anyway."

Things You Gave Up
* diapers
* bottles
* car seats
* holding hands across the street
* action figures
* flash cards
* hanging out in basements
* sleepovers
* spy clubs
* closing eyes when washing hair
* riding dirt bikes
* Trapper Keepers
* keeping lists of girls kissed
* penny loafers
* checking closet and under bed before turning off the light at night
* sports car posters
* musical instruments
* standardized tests
* curfews
* shirts with clothing labels on the outside
* being declared as a dependent on taxes
* virginity

SAVE FOR FIREFLIES

* nicknames
* an ongoing movie scrapbook
* unfettered trust of other human beings
* fear of living in a big city
* idle summers
* nonchalance about money
* the sense that everyone you meet is willing to help you
* wondering if you might be a bachelor the rest of your life
* feeling sorry for yourself
* loneliness
* feeling the need to impress other women in social settings
* your living space not having an impact on someone else
* rock band posters
* not dusting
* weekend nights alone
* English as the only language you'll ever really need
* your own mother and father as the only parental figures in your life
* broad cultural assumptions
* getting by on simply a smile and a nod
* doubt about whether or not your sterile
* not having to plan a year ahead
* idle weekends
* uninterrupted nights
* meals prepared for two
* sleeping in
* the week revolving around own schedule
* hobbies
* thinking of own needs first and foremost
* having nothing to lose

* uninterrupted conversations with spouse
* an uncluttered house
* being able to dry all tears every time
* never losing temper
* having to ride waterslides solo
* counting on beauty alone
* always having someone to look up to
* knowing exactly how long before seeing parents again
* pretending not to be sad when saying goodbye
* thinking home is somewhere else

We exited Pennsylvania, feeling like we were now running on borrowed time. I looked out the back window and noticed Wade had written on the glass with his finger: "WASH ME."

We stopped a diner in Stirling, New Jersey. An elderly man walked by our table on his way out the door. He stooped in slowly toward the four of us and said "I just wanted to say that you have a wonderful family and it has been a pleasure sharing this dining room with you."

This placed the rude, cynical New Jersey stereotype as way off. We'd just met the nicest man in the entire country.

We moved along the roads we traveled at the beginning of the summer, now going in the opposite direction as I ran through the last of my road music, doing my own greatest hits rotation.

Songs and Lyrics That Would Be Forever Wedded to This Trip

* "...can I ignore that sound of distant drumming..." – Just Around the Riverbend, Pocahontas Soundtrack
* "...be safe, you say, whatever the mess you are, you're mine okay..." - Challengers, Neko Case
* "...straight as a razor kickin' the dust, diggin' through ditches and fallin' to rust..." - Rental Car, Beck
* "...drive on, drive on, the highway's bright and long, the rivers overflowing, the houses burning down..." - I Lost You, The Walkmen
* "...a la claire fontaine, m'en allant promener, j'ai trouvé l'eau si belle, que m'y suis baigné..." - A la claire fontaine, popular French children's song
* "...I'll see you in the stars above, in the tall grass and the ones I love..." - You're Gonna Make Me Lonesome When You Go, Bob Dylan
* "...raised in the woods so's he knew every tree, he killed him a 'bar when he was only three..." - Davy Crockett, Tennessee Ernie Ford

We had one more night of camping in one last campground. Swinging through the Hudson River Valley again on the return route toward Boston, we stopped at the Rip Van Winkle Campground in Saugerties, NY. This was, according to the legend, the area where a man lay down against a tree for a nap and slept through the Civil War. Depictions of his bearded countenance were scattered throughout the campground.

But that was where the fun ended. The gruff host at the front desk assigned us a site and handed over three pages of rules to abide, which included no urinating outdoors and no insect repellent allowed. Having covered the full gambit of campgrounds, I shook my head at the seriousness of the staff lording over this patch of woods. I tossed the sheet into the fire, which I would by the end of the evening urinate on.

Cecile stacked up the contents of our camper cabinets and fridge on the site picnic table.

"This is what we need to eat tonight and tomorrow morning."

We had a half a jar of pickles, a half loaf of sliced bread, a jug of cranberry juice, a nearly full bottle of maple syrup, a box of spaghetti, two kinds of cereal, some stale pita bread, five apples, three bananas, two avocadoes, almost thirty marshmallows and a box of Cheez-Its. I'd lost my appetite for most of them. We gave away most of it to the campers at the adjacent site.

After the girls got their feet and pants wet in the muddy creek, I made my last fire. I sat beside it on the picnic bench. I carved my name in the table under the words "East to West to East in 70 days."

Fireflies then crept back out of the darkening woods. I hadn't seen them since the Ozarks, over two months ago. They rose from the overgrown forest floor, as the crickets provided the high 1-2 chirp.

The firefly light came from everywhere. Their blinking would go on like this, whether I stayed to observe it or not.

We pulled into Yann and Sophie's driveway the following afternoon, back to the first stop of our tour when the camper was clean and its driver and navigator weren't sure where we were headed or if we would manage.

The household had a new addition. Their third daughter had been born in late July. It brought into focus the length of our time on the road. Whole new lives had come into existence while we'd been out there. Sophie went from carrying around a weight to carrying a healthy, wide-eyed little person in her arms.

Julie and Louise were calmer on this visit, perhaps understanding they'd made an enormous journey. It merited some pride.

We also celebrated the second birthday of Yann and Sophie's middle daughter who'd hit two. We helped set up and blow balloons for the party that morning. Soon, kids and parents from the neighborhood showed up with gifts and swimwear for their kids.

Standing beside the inflatable pool getting splashed by kids on a birthday-cake sugar high, I met a father of three in a sun-faded Red Sox cap. He gave his background and explained he and his family had just returned the day before from a week on "the Cape."

"What about you? Are you from around here?"

I paused over where to start, one more time. "Well, we drove up yesterday from Pennsylvania." I pointed to our camper that was parked outside the backyard's wooden fence.

"You drove here from Pennsylvania!? You've come a long way then," he said, incredulous.

I waited a moment before explaining the full picture. Distances remained entirely relative.

By the end, we'd thoroughly immersed ourselves in another American pastime: credit card debt. There had been too many temptations along the way, too many food stops and superstores and unique gift shops and one too many nights opting for the hotel.

So, we reasoned, why start holding back now? We ate our last meal in an American restaurant at The Cheesecake Factory in Providence, Rhode Island in view of the dome of the state's capital building. It seemed like a fitting gastronomical end. We opened the novel-size menu to choices from every type of cuisine imaginable from Italian pasta dishes to seafood platters to Mexican and Thai concoctions to American barbeque classics. After the main meal, we were presented with over a hundred different types of cheesecakes available to round the meal out. My pants were by now too tight. I brought my belt buckle back two notches. I gained close to ten pounds over the summer, in a season when I normally lose weight.

By the end of the day, we exited the main highway into Bridgeport and then onto a smaller road beginning in New Haven, Connecticut. This took us through the campus of Yale University.

In a practice field, a group of guys did pushups by the sidelines. The blue and white Bulldog transit buses were partially filled with students who'd arrived early for the semester. Within a week, classes would begin. It felt time for us to get back to that which was serious and fixed.

SAVE FOR FIREFLIES

Our last night was spent in Danbury, Connecticut. In town, we found a Goodwill Thrift Store beside a post office. The items from the camper that we hadn't left with my parents or thrown away, we either donated to Goodwill or mailed back to Dijon. That left us with two large suitcases crammed so full they barely latched closed and four carry-on backpacks.

Later, the hotel swimming pool had a wall size photograph of a forest scene, like an absconded picture I'd taken somewhere along the way that had already been turned into a stock photo. It restated for me that all this was, in fact, already gone. The experience might stay with me, but the clarion majesty would be left where it was.

I was no longer in those woods. I was only gazing at the mock-up.

- - -

Things Found In My Cargo Shorts Pockets Upon Dropping Off the Camper After Ten Weeks on the Road
* wallet and apartment keys
* a purple barrette with a small ballerina figurine affixed to it
* half a roll of Butter Rum-flavored LifeSavers
* a buy-one-get-one-free coupon for a place called Cruizzers Pizza that I'd never seen before
* Swiss army knife
* an unused Chicago metro ticket
* a nearly empty bottle of orange-scented hand sanitizer
* a dimming flashlight
* 43 cents in dimes, nickels and pennies

* a widening hole
* the back of manager Ernst's business card, where I wrote down the final number on the camper odometer: 11,758 miles

The driver escorted us back to JFK airport. We passed the New York City skyline crossing the Bronx-Whitestone Bridge. The colossal buildings stood right up against the river's edge. The World Trade Center Towers' absence was still sharply apparent to me. The two bookends on the southern tip had been erased from the sky and from the vision I'd always held as fixed.

Over the East River, New York looked like an unattainable island, one that couldn't possibly hold all that had been built upon it. Looking beyond its skyscrapers, I saw the Shenandoah Valley and the Cascade Mountains, the wilderness and the downtowns, the neon of Vegas and the starlight of Bryce Canyon, the heated pools and the frigid rivers, old friends I no longer knew and complete strangers who understood everything, the warm, familiar homes and the unsettling culture shock, the optimism and the decline, the sand and the woods, the gas gauge and the dotted white line, the bellow of foghorns and the blinking of fireflies.

Simone de Beauvoir described it, again, better than I could. "I've done it. I've seen the Grand Canyon. The sparkling hope that I nursed for so long has changed into the definite past. For all my expectations, I'm left with one memory, only memory."

We would be left with only memory too. But we'd return on the persistent promise that the country was still young and renewing itself daily, starting here from the ground of New York City up. We'd return knowing how much we had yet to see.

But we would go back to our lives in France without doubts, about where we wanted to be and about the future. We'd remain in this smaller, older, more manageable country for the moment.

Cecile, after deliberation, chose to stay with her job. We would continue to have the courage to be unconventional, to be a mother who works long days, with high pressure and a long commute, and to be a father who keeps the whirling home life in balance in a language that continued to confound him. The girls would together keep the unique blend of their dual influences.

My nostalgia for whatever I may have left behind was cured, perhaps momentarily, but cured all the same. I'd done enough looking back. For once, I'd caught up that much. I wouldn't need to cradle this memory so delicately.

In the next year, a friend of mine from York took a trip to Paris. She had been looking forward to it all year. Upon arrival she got in touch with me and told me what a gorgeous city it was, how amazing it must be to live here and how everything in France was positively dream-like.

She was deluded and seeing things through rose-colored glasses. And she was completely right.

Later that Fall, my father-in-law inquired with me about how one goes about renting a motorcycle in the U.S. "It is a dream of mine ever since I was a boy to take a trip on a Harley Davidson in America."

SAVE FOR FIREFLIES

The news from the United States in the Fall of 2008 offered another narrative. The stock market had its worst crash in decades that October. The default mortgage crisis turned up even more nightmarish than anticipated. Unemployment numbers soared.

My Dad, months later, would be laid off from his longtime employer. He'd been phased out his job and his career.

On the first week of November, Americans elected Barack Hussein Obama as their president. I watched on France's TF1 as he and his family took the stage in Chicago's Grant Park to shouts and screams and tears of joy. A feeling of immense promise, followed swiftly by a measure of the enormity of his task ahead, swelled even in the French press.

Across Europe, everyone knew how to say "Yes, we can" in English. From the political blog the Daily Dish, Andrew Sullivan quoted from Alexis de Tocqueville's *De la démocratie en Amérique*: "The greatness of America lies not in being more enlightened than any other nation, but rather in her ability to repair her faults."

Over and over visitors from France to America and vice versa, continue to see their dreams come true when they first land on this foreign soil.

They were caught up in an illusion. They saw the country they visited with more clarity than the native.

The question remained: which country held the dream for me?

REVENIR (ONE MORE TIME) - - -

A whole season had passed without us. Leaves on the neighborhood trees that had just sprouted before our trip, now dangled yellow in a crisper air. Friends' children had grown taller. New storefronts had emerged on Dijon's streets. Meanwhile, we had two full plastic bags of mail collected by my in-laws and an unwashed coffee cup that we'd left in the kitchen sink on the morning before catching our flight which had acquired a thick greenish brown mold, an isolated vision of neglect.

We went to the park in the center of Dijon that day after our trip, still lost as to what time it actually was. Cecile had another two weeks of sabbatical left. Julie didn't start school for another week. And I had no writing projects in the pipeline.

Louise, however, was the one who was ready to get back to business. The day after returning to Dijon, we all shuffled lethargically through the park, not sure what we were supposed to be doing here. Louise climbed the stairs on the ladder that scared her last time in this park. She reached the top, settled herself into the sitting launch position and zipped down the slide.

She raised her hands in the air at the end, less in triumph than in a gesture that said: "It's as simple as that."

Is this how we lived? Was this how I washed the dishes? And, more importantly, why? Jet lag leaves you neither here nor there, and by the time you've grown impatient waiting for the answer to your questions about your former daily habits, that hollowness of displacement has disappeared. One might expect me to simply say it wore off, like the jet lag. In these moments, the emptiness and waywardness can't be pushed out by the familiar. I wish I didn't have to call this maturing.

So I opened the windows in my daughter's room to close the shutters for the night and looked to the west where the sun set. The pink light held the silhouettes of the small ceramic chimneys lining the tops of stone buildings. It was the oldest manmade thing I'd seen in months.

On the first days back, with suitcases still laying open, waiting to be relieved of the dirty clothes and sand from a California beach sieved to the bottom, home doesn't feel like anything without wheels. The jet lag reinforces this feeling and augments the disorientation. We are not here. We are not there. I stare out our bedroom window with an ear toward the girls in their rooms already asleep until I am ready to join them. I lie in the bed I remember from four months ago, but which is somehow not ours yet.

I wake up the next day and the next day again finally feeling caught up, but then missing the jet lag, or the road lag, that pull of the counted mile markers that spurred our crossing of all the highways, but which I must try to make a memory of now as well.

Despite knowing better, I don't want to get over it just yet. I don't want to know exactly where my home is.

SAVE FOR FIREFLIES

I want instead an exit sign that tells me something lies ahead I should see and I want the wheels to be already in motion so that getting there takes only a rightward dip of my steering wheel. I want to find the road blocked by bison or find the pavement washed over with white sand.

I want my daughters to be there, already well ahead of me.

About the Author

Nathaniel Missildine lives in Dijon, France with his wife and two daughters. His first novel, *Far North*, was published in 2006 as an ebook by Pulpbits, Inc. Other writings are collected at www.nathanielmissildine.com